THE ONLY TRUE PEOPLE

Pueblo Woman, Taos Pueblo, New Mexico

Colorado Historical Society

THE ONLY TRUE PEOPLE

A History of the
Native Americans of the Colorado Plateau

by Kathleene Parker

THUNDER MESA PUBLISHING

COVER: *Navajo Man by William M. Pennington*
Courtesy Colorado Historical Society

BACK COVER: *Old Navajo Man by William M. Pennington*
Courtesy Durango Public Library

ISBN 0-9625717-0-9

Design: Candus Clark and Kathleene Parker

Editor: Kathleene Parker

Maps and Graphics: Candus Clark

Typesetting: Avenir ® Corporation, Denver

Printing: Walsworth Press Company, Inc.; Marceline, Missouri.

Copyright © 1991 by Thunder Mesa Publishing

Acknowledgements

We wish to give special thanks to author/publisher F.A. Barnes of
Moab, Utah, without whose valuable advice and direction this
book probably would not have become reality.

ABOUT THE AUTHOR

Kathleene Parker grew up on the Colorado Plateau, where three
different families of her ancestors were early settlers. She edited
an award-winning newspaper in Durango, Colorado, for several
years and more recently edited a regional newspaper focusing on
environmental and energy issue of the American West for the
Denver Public Library. She has written extensively about the
natural and cultural history of the Colorado Plateau region.

Dedication

To Mel and Kassidy.
In memory of Theo and Pearl Parker, Jean McCulloch, and Dell
Tinnin.—"It is finished (again) in beauty."

Anasazi Pottery

Mesa Verde National Park

CONTENTS

Laguna Pueblo, New Mexico

William H. Jackson, Colorado Historical Society

Preface

Almost universally among the indigenous people of the Colorado Plateau region, and for that matter among most other of the indigenous people of North America, the individual Indian tribes have names for themselves which, in various languages and in various ways, mean basically, "The People," "The Human Beings," or in some cases, "The Only True People,"

Somehow the name *The Only True People* seemed particularly appropriate for a book about the indigenous people of the Colorado Plateau, because they are after all the original citizens—the true people—of that beautiful and scenic land. While we make no claim that *The Only True People* is an authoritative source, it nonetheless strives to provide a general overview, from a historical perspective, of the amazingly beautiful and sometimes phenomenally complex indigenous cultures of the Colorado Plateau region of the American Southwest.

And in that light, we hope that the reader will bear in mind the importance of judging the cultures of the indigenous people of the Americas based solely on their own merit. Since Columbus arrived in the Western Hemisphere five hundred years ago, indigenous cultures have been unfairly compared with and measured by the standards of European cultures, a bias which has largely deprived the world of the opportunity to be enlightened by their beauty and accomplishments.

The world as a whole, as much as the indigenous people, has suffered as a result. Hardly a high school student, for example, has not learned of the historic city of Rome but remained ignorant of ancient Western Hemisphere cities of equal or greater size and accomplishment. If a direct analogy is required, the conquest of the Americas can be compared to the implications of an alien race conquering the Earth and, in so doing, assuming that all that humanity has accomplished is worthless and in need of replacement by their own "superior" ways.

Thus, regrettably, most people know little about the various Indian tribes, their beliefs, their histories, their viewpoints, their religions, or the quandary they face as they are caught between two often diametrically opposing ways of life.

And now a word about the historic photographs used in this book. Not only do we owe a debt of gratitude to the personnel of the various museums, national parks, and libraries from which the photos were obtained, but we especially wish to acknowledge the talent, the dedication, the determination, and the unbending resolve of those who photographed the indigenous people of the Colorado Plateau during the late nineteenth and early twentieth centuries. The photographs in this book include those of famous photographer William H. Jackson, who journeyed throughout much of the unexplored West in the 1860s and 1870s making the first photographic record of many of its people and much of its landscape, and William M. Pennington, who lived in Durango, Colorado, and who had an uncanny knack for capturing both the drama and the tragedy of the Navajo people. Also included are photographs taken by the John Wesley Powell Expedition of 1871 and 1872, which traveled through some of the most rugged terrain on Earth as it journeyed down the Colorado River through the Grand Canyon.

Because of its formidable terrain, many areas of the Colorado Plateau, even today, remain isolated. A century ago, most regions could be reached only on foot, on horseback, or occasionally by wagon. More, the cameras and film plates with which photographers then worked were heavy and cumbersome, often requiring a mule or a horse-drawn wagon just for their collective transport. Photography of the indigenous people, therefore, often meant an act of sheer will and determination, but thanks to the efforts of such determined photographers part of the region's richest heritage was recorded for posterity.

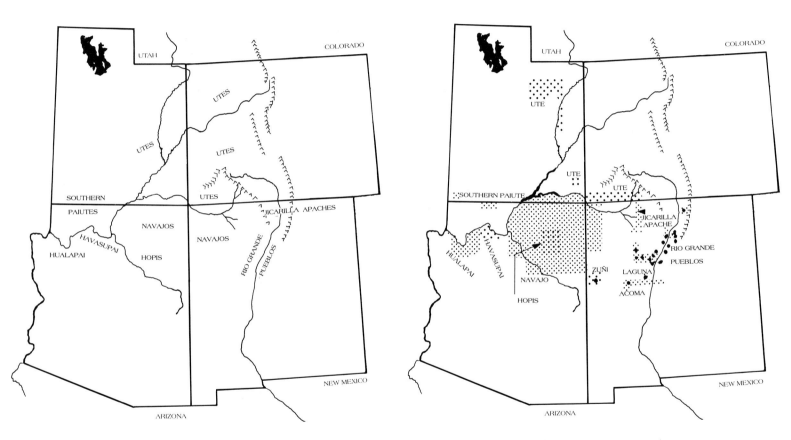

Indigenous Lands

Present-Day Reservations

Monument Valley Navajo Tribal Park, Arizona

Kathleene Parker

The Land

The Colorado Plateau is not a plateau in the conventional sense of the word. It is instead an enormous geologic province sprawled across 150,000 square miles of central and southern Utah, northern Arizona, western Colorado, and northwestern New Mexico. It holds scenery classic to the American West. People from throughout the world envision its towering desert monuments, yawning sheer-walled canyons, and sagebrush- and prickly pear-dotted mesas when they think of "The West," or more specifically, "The Southwest."

The Colorado Plateau is one of the most scenic and colorful regions in the world. Over twenty United States national parks and monuments, the so-called Golden Circle of National Parks, rest upon its expanses. Two of these, Mesa Verde and Grand Canyon national parks, number among only a few World Heritage Sites recognized by the United Nations Educational, Scientific, and Cultural Organization in consideration of natural and cultural features of global preeminence. The Grand Canyon is also listed as one of the Seven Natural Wonders of the World.

Because inexorable geologic forces long ago lifted the Colorado Plateau region thousands of feet higher than surrounding lands, the Painted Desert, which rests upon its heights, is often referred to as "the high desert." Even most of the plateau's lower regions rest at over five thousand feet above sea level, and the peaks of its desert mountains—the La Sals, the Abajos, the Henrys, the Chuskas, the Lukachukais, the Carrizos, the San Francisco Peaks, Navajo Mountain, Sleeping Ute

Mountain, and Mount Taylor—often exceed ten thousand and twelve thousand feet. Southwestern Colorado's towering San Juan Mountains, meanwhile, which some geologists consider to be, by some definitions, part of

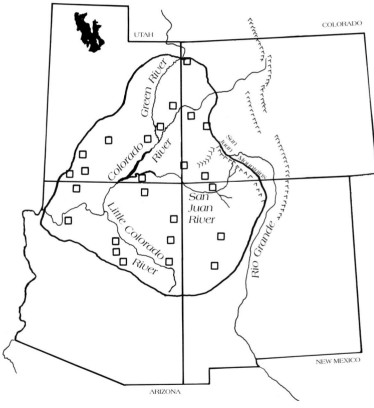

Colorado Plateau   (Squares Indicate National Parks and Monuments)

the Colorado Plateau, exceed fourteen thousand feet.

The Colorado Plateau forms much of the drainage area of the Colorado River, the principle river of the southwestern United States. The waters of the Colorado and its major tributaries, the Green, the Little Colorado, and the San Juan, as well as countless other smaller tributaries, have been the major erosional force shaping the Colorado Plateau during the past ten million years. As the Colorado Plateau uplifted, the rivers and streams cut downward, ultimately carving the stupendous canyons of Arizona, Colorado, and Utah and shaping the rest of the Colorado Plateau into one of the most magnificent landscapes on the planet.

The Colorado Plateau is a land that often seems contradictory, one moment ruthless and inhospitable, the next gentle and unthinkably beautiful.

Raking winds, especially in the spring, fan immense clouds of dust high into the sky. Great, torrential rains—borne of monsoons arriving in late summer ladened with moisture from off the distant Pacific and the Gulf of Mexico—sometimes send flashfloods roaring down usually dry ravines. And in much of this mile-high land, snow or killing frosts may occur into late May or early June, only to return as early as September.

But there is a soft, tender side to the land too.

The fragrance of sage and piñon permeate the air and ephemeral rainbows span mighty canyons in the coolness after the great summer storms. Tiny hummingbirds sip nectar from flowers growing near desert seeps, while tablelands shimmer lavender in the heat-distorted distance.

And upon this extraordinary land live American Indians—they prefer to be called Native Americans—the indigenous people of the Colorado Plateau. Their cultures evolved here over thousands of years to become arguably some of the most colorful and unique in the world.

They are the Ute, Paiute, Navajo, Jicarilla Apache, Pai, and Pueblo peoples, distinct tribal groups with widely disparate histories, different languages (Native Americans in the United States and Canada at one time spoke over 250 different languages.) different religions, and different customs. The way of life of each tribe has been molded over the centuries by the domineering influence of the beautiful but harsh land upon which they live, an adversity which made their cultures both colorful and resilient. Simply by living in this place, the Native Americans of the Colorado Plateau cause a land of already unfathomable beauty to be even more alluring and beautiful and mysterious.

Part One
Prehistory

Anasazi Pottery

Mesa Verde National Park

Monument Valley Navajo Tribal Park

Kathleene Parker

The Beginning

The Native American people of the Colorado Plateau and many other American Indians were living in the Americas thousands of years before the European explorer Columbus "discovered" the New World in 1492.

When humankind actually arrived in the Western Hemisphere has to date been obscured among the secrets of remote antiquity. The earliest conclusively proven human habitations, found in Colorado, New Mexico, and Arizona, date from around eleven thousand years ago, while evidence of earlier habitation remains controversial.

Humankind probably arrived from Asia sometime toward the end of the Pleistocene glacial period, fifteen thousand to thirty thousand years ago. That ice age, beginning about two million years ago, brought four major glacial advances, each of which covered nearly all of Canada with ice.

During colder weather and the resulting ice advances, enormous amounts of sea water were locked into glaciers, causing the sea level to drop. This may have exposed a land bridge across the Bering Sea between Asia and Alaska, over which people traveled toward the end of the final glacial advance of the Pleistocene Ice Age, the Wisconsin glaciation. As warmer weather opened a corridor through the Canadian ice field, these people of Mongolian, or central-Asian, descent were probably subsequently able to find a way south into the heart of the continent. Through the time span of many hundreds of years, the descendants of these early people migrated across the expanses of all of North and South America and developed distinct cultures borne of environment, experience, and circumstance.

Archeologists now call the first known inhabitants of the southwestern United States, including the Colorado Plateau, "Paleo Indians." Hunters and gatherers, these early people followed the movement of animals, including the great beasts such as cave bears, long-horned bison, mammoths, camels, horses, ground sloths, and mastodons.

However, between 8,000 B.C. and 10,000 B.C., a radical decline in precipitation associated with the end of the Wisconsin glaciation triggered a massive drought, especially in the Southwest. This, perhaps along with excessive hunting and the spread of disease, led to the extinction of most of the big animals upon which the Paleo Indians had depended. As a result many Paleo Indians followed surviving game animals eastward out of the Southwest onto the more hospitable Great Plains. There the Paleo Indian hunting tradition survived well into historical times.

As many of the Paleo Indians left the Southwest, they were gradually replaced by people of what archeologists call the "Desert Archaic" culture of Mexico, California, and the basin regions of the American West. The Desert Archaic culture dominated all of the Southwest, including the Colorado Plateau, from 6,000 B.C. to about 1 A.D. From that culture, which not only hunted animals that had survived the Pleistocene-era extinctions, but put greater emphasis on gathering plants, emerged many, but not all, of the colorful indigenous cultures of today's Colorado Plateau.

The Desert Archaic peoples moved across the land

in what anthropologists call the "seasonal round," an annual migration during which they followed larger animals such as deer and elk into the high country in summer and back into the lower valleys and desert in the autumn. During this migration, they killed large and small animals and harvested wild fruits, berries, seeds, roots, grasses, and grains.

About four thousand years ago, a primitive form of pod corn, the ancestor to maize, was brought into the Southwest from deep in Mexico, and the Desert Archaic people made a subtle but important modification in their way of life.

As they began their seasonal round in the spring, they planted corn, a plant then found exclusively in the Americas, in protected lower canyons and valleys. When they returned in the fall, they harvested whatever crop had been produced by the untended plants. Soon, they were also planting squash, and by about three thousand years ago, at least in the southern areas of the Southwest, beans. What archeologists and anthropologists call the "sacred triad"—corn, beans, and squash—the mainstay of the Native American agriculture, had arrived. Gradually, over centuries, these agricultural crops became increasingly important to the Desert people, who in many cases began to modify their migration habits so that they had more time to plant and to tend their crops.

Contrary to popular belief, however, the hunter-gatherers were loath to become farmers. They enjoyed a bountiful natural harvest assembled with little effort, a fact testified to by repeated attempts by some prehistoric farmers to quit farming and return to a strictly hunting-gathering economy. Even during modern times, primitive hunting-gathering people invest far fewer working hours each day than do urban dwellers.

Probably solely motivated by the pragmatic need to find more dependable food supplies, as population growth or other factors strained naturally occurring food supplies, at least some of the Desert Archaic people made the slow transition from wanderers to settled farmers, and the foundation was established upon which remarkably advanced societies were eventually built.

Empires of the Ancients

The accomplishments of the pre-Columbian people of North and South America are often forgotten or underestimated. Yet, just as empires rose and fell in the Eastern Hemisphere for centuries prior to Columbus, so too had they risen and fallen in the Americas.

And what made these civilizations especially astounding was the fact that they were built solely through human toil. Unlike Europe, Asia, the Middle East, and Africa, the Americas had few animals suitable for domestication. There were no beasts of burden, except perhaps the dog in North America, and only the llama and alpaca, capable of carrying only relatively small loads, in South America. Therefore, the civilizations of the pre-Columbian indigenous people of North America moved forward on human muscle alone, often to phenomenal heights.

Moreover, because there were few animals suitable

for agricultural use in the Americas and because only limited types of grains were available for cultivation compared with abundant arable grains found throughout Europe and Asia, the people of the Americas were at a nutritional disadvantage. In addition, with the north-to-south orientation of the two continents, temperate zones in North America are widely isolated from temperate zones in South America, limiting the diffusion of arable plants from one region to another. In the prehistoric Americas, for example, the potato never spread northward from its native Andes, while similar plants spread rapidly across thousands of miles of climatically similar Europe and Asia.

Therefore, because geography, environment, and climate—those things which most directly mold the course of human events—were so radically different, it is probably unscientific to compare pre-Columbian America with pre-Columbian Europe. It is enough to say that each carved its own niche, with the Americas reaching their own unique levels of glory.

Thirty miles northeast of Mexico City, for example, rest the ruins of the city of Teotihuacan. Founded about 1 A.D., it eventually grew to over 200,000 people and covered eight square miles, making it larger than the imperial city of Rome. Before Teotihuacan mysteriously burned and was abandoned about 750 A.D., its citizens commanded a trading empire stretching north into what is now the southwestern United States and south as far as Honduras and El Salvador.

Centuries later there were the astounding empires of the Incas in Peru, the Aztecs in Mexico, and the Mayans in Central America. The greatness of those civilizations was perhaps illustrated by accomplishments such as the Mayan development of the concept of zero and cities such as the Aztec city of Tenochtitlan, now Mexico City. It was constructed on an island in the middle of a shallow lake and was reached by causeways. Shortly after Columbus's arrival in the New World, Tenochtitlan had a population approaching 300,000 people, approximately five times larger than London at the same time. The beautiful city was surrounded by great floating gardens cultivated upon mats floating upon the lake's surface and used to feed the city's burgeoning population. Of it the Spanish explorer Díaz said, "...the great towers and temples and buildings...there were even some of our soldiers who asked if what they saw was in a dream...."

And improbably, far to the north upon the often inhospitable expanses of Colorado Plateau, another civilization had arisen a few hundred years earlier, enigmatic and beautiful and awe inspiring in its own right.

Restored Great Kiva, Aztec Ruins National Monument

Mel Burnett

The Anasazi

About 2500 years ago, embers of what was to eventually become an impressive civilization began to smolder on the Colorado Plateau. Originating out of the Desert Archaic tradition, that civilization finally burst into full flame, only to mysteriously falter a thousand years later. Amazingly, though, a living, vibrant remnant of this ancient culture still survives in the southwestern United States.

The people of this long-ago civilization are known today as the Anasazi, from the Navajo word, *Anaasází*, which has been variously interpreted to mean "Ancient Tribe," "Ancient Ones," or "Enemy Ancestors." What the Anasazi called themselves, however, will probably always remain one of the lost secrets of antiquity.

They were a reddish-brown-haired or black-haired people of short, stalky stature. They lived primarily along the San Juan River drainage area of the Colorado Plateau, a region now known as the Four Corners area because the borders of four states, Colorado, New Mexico, Arizona, and Utah, intersect there. However, theirs and related cultures also existed as far away as Nevada and central Arizona.

The first evidence in the Four Corners area of the Anasazi as a distinct, identifiable group differing from other Desert Archaic people dates from about 500 B.C. Finally, sometime before 500 A.D., the first known permanent Anasazi village was built to the north of the current-day town of Durango, Colorado, in a fertile, gentle valley cradled in the southern foothills of the San Juan Mountains and intersected by the deep, rolling waters of the Animas River.

Like other Desert Archaic people, the Anasazi had been hunter-gatherers, who planted crops to augment natural food supplies. Eventually, however, they settled down in order to devote more energy to cultivation. Over a period of a couple of centuries, many communities consisting of "pithouses"—rounded little dwellings resting partly above ground, partly below ground, and roofed with logs and a mud-and-clay mixture that archeologists call "wattle-and-daub"—sprang up throughout the Four Corners area. Special pithouses, meanwhile, today known as *kivas* (Hopi for "sacred ceremonial chamber"), were built in the villages for use as religious structures.

This earliest stage of Anasazi development, the Basketmaker era, was so named because while the still-primitive people wove extremely intricate baskets and sandals, they lacked the ability to make pottery. The Basketmaker Anasazi cultivated fields of squash and corn near their pithouses and hunted wild animals and harvested wild plants across the broad expanse of foothills, plateaus, and canyons of the Colorado Plateau.

But by roughly 750 A.D., the Animas Valley and most other valleys were abandoned by the Anasazi, perhaps because of a period of damp summer weather that simultaneously made the river valleys cooler and more flood prone and the warmer mesa tops and desert more arable.

Between 500 A.D. and 700 A.D., the Anasazi began to cultivate beans, and by about 750 A.D., depending upon the individual community, since theirs was not a homogeneous society, the Anasazi culture began to flare into full intensity. It was the beginning of what is now

Diorama of Mesa Verde Pithouses

Colorado Historical Society

known as the Developmental Pueblo era.

It was then that the Anasazi began to make pottery and move their dwellings from the earth into the sun, as they abandoned their pithouses and instead constructed *pueblos* (Spanish for "village" or "town"), the beginning of a building tradition still in use across the American Southwest. The early pueblos, made of stone bonded with mud mortar, were simple rectangular-shaped, one-story structures, abutting one another, sharing one or two common walls, and usually facing south or southwest. The kivas of the Developmental Pueblo era, meanwhile, were moved deeper into the ground than their pithouse predecessors, were made somewhat larger, and were made with masonry and mortar walls, rather than wattle-and-daub.

Over the next few hundred years, the pueblos gradually became much more elaborate until between 1100 A.D. (much earlier in one instance) and 1300 A.D.—about the time Christians in distant Europe were launching the Crusades—they evolved into great multi-stories complexes of the Great, or Classic, Pueblo era.

And the Anasazi people of this time refined other skills, developing pottery with intricate designs in a multitude of colors; weaving fabrics out of cotton, perhaps grown by the Anasazi or perhaps purchased from people living in Arizona and central New Mexico; making elaborate jewelry of turquoise; extending systems of trade across hundreds of miles of the prehistoric Southwest and even deep into Mexico; refining methods of agriculture; and developing a complex religion integrated into every aspect of their lives.

The height of the Anasazi civilization had arrived.

The Chaco Phenomenon

The ruins of literally hundreds of long-ago Anasazi villages today dot the expanses of the Colorado Plateau. From the deep, secluded canyons of Utah and Arizona, to the lush, green foothills of Colorado's San Juan Mountains, to the sunburned desert of northwestern New Mexico, vestiges of sometimes awesome communities glisten in the Southwestern sun.

A thousand or more years ago, these communities began to flourish, not part of an extensive, closely knit, bureaucratic empire, but each a loosely bonded part of a cultural amalgam. The Anasazi people of widely disparate geographic regions probably didn't even speak the same languages, although they shared many other basic cultural traits. Individual communities, often isolated by great miles of Southwestern landscape, evolved and changed, motivated by the specific environmental, social, and cultural conditions indigenous to each geographic region. The complexity to which each evolved was in direct relation to the wealth of the land. Some rocketed to greatness in a few short centuries, others plodded along unspectacularly, but dependably, to persevere rather than excel.

Archeologists today recognize three major, distinct variations of the Anasazi culture, each named for the geographic locale where it evolved: the Chaco Canyon, Mesa Verde, and Kayenta cultural groups. There were

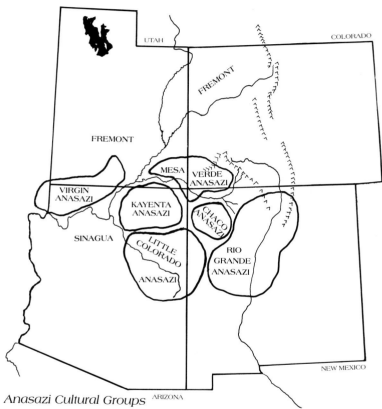

Anasazi Cultural Groups

the upper Rio Grande River and its tributaries and along the drainage area of the eastern Rio Puerco between present-day Grants and Albuquerque, New Mexico. However, these three were less archeologically distinctive than the Chaco Canyon, Mesa Verde, and Kayenta cultural groups.

While Mesa Verde is today the most famous of all Anasazi sites, it was in fact at Chaco Canyon, New Mexico, today preserved as Chaco Culture National Historic Park, that the Anasazi built the zenith of their civilization. But the Chaco culture, which rose like a mighty nova across the sky long before other Anasazi cultural centers, also darkened and died first, standing empty and abandoned while many of the Mesa Verde and Kayenta pueblos and cliff dwellings were still being built.

Chaco Canyon rests almost exactly in the middle of the dry, sun-blistered San Juan Basin, a roughly twenty-six thousand square-mile subsidence in the land that occurred as the San Juan Mountains were pushed skyward some miles to the north sixty million years ago. Chaco Canyon is little more than a parched, rock-strewn ravine through which the Rio Chaco flows, usually nothing more than a feeble trickle of water moving west, then north, toward the San Juan River.

By 900 A.D., around two centuries earlier than Anasazi elsewhere, the Chaco people were at the height of the Great Pueblo era. Enormous pueblos were built along a roughly twenty-mile-long section of Chaco Canyon near Fajada Butte, a solitary desert monument protruding from the relative flatness of the San Juan

three other cultural groups, the Virgin River Anasazi, in extreme southwestern Utah and northwestern Arizona north of the Grand Canyon; the Little Colorado Anasazi, to the southeast of the Grand Canyon along the Arizona-New Mexico border; and the Rio Grande Anasazi, along

Basin. Here, the Chaco Anasazi used elaborate water-control systems to carefully divert the region's marginal precipitation onto their crops.

Thirteen enormous pueblos, called "great houses," sometimes housing a thousand or more people each, stood at Chaco Canyon by 1000 A.D., reaching a combined peak population of about seven thousand people.

But the most awe-inspiring of all the pueblos was Pueblo Bonito, which means "Beautiful Village" in Spanish.

Artist's Rendering of Pueblo Bonito

Colorado Historical Society

Construction on Pueblo Bonito began in 919 A.D. and continued for roughly 150 years. The pueblo eventually covered over three acres of ground, was four-stories high, contained eight hundred to nine hundred rooms, and housed upwards of a thousand people. Nearby Chetro Ketl (a Navajo term, which has never been precisely translated) was of roughly equivalent size. These two great houses comprised the most advanced pre-Columbian architecture in the United States.

And there were kivas, dozens of them, including "great kivas," enormous religious structures up to sixty-three feet across and vastly different from the average ten- or twelve-foot-across kiva. Casa Rinconada and Kin Nahasbas, standing independent of any pueblo, as well as great kivas within the actual pueblos, could probably easily accommodate a hundred or more worshippers each. They were often constructed partly or entirely above ground, although in some pueblos, they were recessed into the pueblo superstructure in such a way as to give the illusion of being mostly below ground.

But part of the beauty of the Chacoan structures was not just their impressive size, but the intricate detail of construction. The stone work on Bonito-phase buildings—the most advanced Chacoan architecture—consisted of hundreds of thousands of carefully selected, finished, and chinked stones fitted to form a veneer over a center core of earth and stone rubble. Nearly a million such stones were meticulously fitted into the walls of Pueblo Bonito, detail work that seems unjustified since the stone veneer was then hidden beneath plaster.

And the Chaco Anasazi apparently welcomed other

Anasazi into the canyon to live, although perhaps only on a seasonal basis to trade. Many ruins contemporary to Pueblo Bonito and Chetro Ketl, for example, were constructed by Anasazi from McElmo Canyon, Colorado, some one hundred miles northwest of Chaco Canyon and part of the Mesa Verde culture.

And the Chacoans constructed the only known major network of prehistoric roads north of Mexico.

Meticulously built of stone or sometimes by removing soils to expose slickrock formations, these baffling roads swept out across the San Juan Basin, straight and true regardless of terrain. Their combined mileage may have exceeded five hundred miles.

The width, as much as the length, however, forms the real mystery of these prehistoric roads, originally photographed from the air by Charles Lindberg in the 1920s as part of a routine archeological survey, although recognized as highways as long ago as the early 1900s. The main arterial highways were roughly thirty-feet wide, while smaller tributary highways were about half that, strangely wide for people without herd animals or wheeled vehicles.

These highways may provide the answer to one of the most baffling questions confronting archeologists: Why did the Chaco culture, the pinnacle of Anasazi civilization, thrive in one of the driest, most inhospitable areas of the United States?

Archeologists theorize that the ancient highways may have been a lifeline, at least for a time.

While the center of the Chaco culture was Chaco Canyon, archeologists have discovered that at least forty communities scattered around the San Juan Basin were also constructed by the Chaco Anasazi. Among the largest of these "outliers" were two communities about thirty miles to the north, near the present-day town of Aztec, New Mexico. Now known as the Salmon Ruin and Aztec Ruins National Monument, both were of significant size, consisting of elaborate labyrinths of rooms, as well as many kivas, including great kivas.

One of the main characteristics of the Chaco outliers was that they were usually in areas of reliable water supplies. Aztec Ruins National Monument, for example, rests on the banks of the Animas River, one of the largest rivers in the arid San Juan Basin. The people of this northern community cultivated large expanses of crops on fertile lands near the river, as do current-day farmers in the area.

During the early years of the Chaco communities, the Chacoans probably were able to grow adequate crops, even in the semi-arid Chaco environment. As their population expanded, however, the Chaco Anasazi probably had to depend upon distant farmlands, as well as supplies of differing types from other communities. Near Dolores, Colorado, for example, another Chaco outlier, the Escalante Ruin, was recently excavated. Located near the high mountains and containing large amounts of bone fragments, it may have been a Chaco hunting outpost. Meanwhile, huge timber beams used as roof supports in the great houses and great kivas—over 200,000 roof beams at Chaco alone—salt, and other imported goods probably ultimately entered Chaco Canyon along its elaborate system of roads. These imports were often purchased from neighboring Anasazi, as well as from people as distant as the Pacific coast, the Sea of Cortez, and Mexico.

The Chacoans probably paid for such commodities with turquoise, a semi-precious stone mined by the Chacoans near Mount Taylor, along the southern rim of the San Juan Basin. The Chacoans often inlaid turquoise into wood, bone, or stone pendants and bracelets; into craft items, such as mosaic sets; or into beaded necklaces, created by boring small holes through tiny pieces of turquoise then strung into multi-strand necklaces.

And the Chacoans were people of the sun.

Beyond its size and intricate construction detail, Pueblo Bonito was oriented to utilize solar heating. Virtually every inhabited room within the crescent-shaped pueblo received direct sunlight each day. Strange corner doorways and windows were also probably used to track the movement of the sun on the horizon and thus foretell the approaching solstices and other important religious observances.

And near the top of Fajada Butte, the Anasazi chiselled two spirals onto a rock surface behind three slabs of native sandstone that rest at an angle against the outcropping. Sunlight, shining between the rocks onto the carefully placed spirals, marks the spring and fall equinox and the summer and winter solstices, forming an amazingly accurate solar calendar. Archeologists, however, are uncertain if the calendar was used to predict solstices or if it was simply a religious shrine to the sun.

The Kayenta Cities

Roughly 150 miles west, northwest of Chaco Canyon in northern Arizona, the ruins of three incredibly beautiful Anasazi communities nestle in or near a seemingly out of place aspen-filled canyon, Tsegi Canyon, in the very heart of the Painted Desert. This region, near today's town of Kayenta, Arizona, was the center of the Kayenta Anasazi culture, which blossomed much later than the Chacoan culture but also survived much longer

The Kayenta people lived not only at Tsegi Canyon, to the southwest of Monument Valley, but were also scattered across much of nearby Black Mesa. They also lived in the depths of the Grand Canyon, along many of the canyons of the lower San Juan River system at Glen Canyon, and along the Escalante River in extreme southern Utah.

But the three Kayenta towns at Tsegi Canyon—Betatakin (with 150 rooms the largest cliff dwelling in Arizona), Keet Seel, and Inscription House—represent the height of the Kayenta culture and are preserved today as Navajo National Monument. Betatakin nestles under an enormous sweep of Navajo sandstone that forms a sheltering overhang. Built about 1250 A.D., Betatakin is, because of its setting, one of the most beautiful cliff dwellings in the Southwest.

Although near the Colorado, Little Colorado, and San Juan rivers, the people of the Kayenta district in fact lived on one of the driest part of the Colorado Plateau and probably found life to be much more difficult than did their counterparts at Chaco Canyon. Unlike the Chaco Anasazi, they were far removed from the relatively moist, fertile regions bordering the arid San Juan Basin. Thus, they were probably preoccupied with the simple business of survival and had little time to achieve architectural and cultural excellence.

Nonetheless, their towns were beautiful, both because of construction and setting. Yet, the various Anasazi architectural stages were not chronologically delineated in the Kayenta district as they were in other cultural centers. It was not uncommon, for example, for some Kayenta Anasazi to live in pithouses next to others living in multi-story pueblos.

Probably the single most outstanding achievement of the Kayenta Anasazi was the development of vividly colored polychrome pottery. Black, white, and red geometric designs were laid down over yellow or orange backgrounds.

And while the Chaco Anasazi seemed preoccupied with building many kivas and extremely large kivas, the Kayenta Anasazi built only comparatively few religious structures and these were humble. At Betatakin, for example, the Kayentans used only square, above-ground ceremonial structures, called *kihus*, rather than traditional kivas.

But though it may not have been as dynamic, the Kayenta culture persevered, surviving long after Chaco Canyon had grown empty and silent.

The Montelores Empire

Stretching from the current-day towns of Monticello and Blanding, Utah, on the west to Cortez and Dolores, Colorado, on the east is one of the most fertile areas in the Southwest. This, the Montelores Plateau, sometimes also called the Great Sage Plain, is a four-thousand square-mile area tilted slightly south into the warming rays of the sun, a circumstance which prolongs the area's growing season in a land infamous for short summers.

Not only is the soil, blown here by prevailing winds from across hundreds of miles of surrounding lands, extremely fertile, but the Montelores Plateau benefits from its proximity to the San Juan Mountains, receiving much more precipitation than most of the rest of the Colorado Plateau as storms bank up against the mountains. Today, although perhaps climatically somewhat less favorable than during the time of the Anasazi, the Montelores Plateau is still an abundant farming region.

Immediately to the southeast and towering some two thousand feet higher than the Montelores Plateau is the Mesa Verde.

On clear star-spackled nights a thousand years ago, the early Anasazi living upon the high Mesa Verde plateau may have been able to see the signal fires of their progressive neighbors at Chaco Canyon, some seventy-five miles to the southeast. Resting between the San Juan Mountains on the north and the Painted Desert to the south and the west, Mesa Verde commands a spectacular view of much of the San Juan Basin and lands beyond.

Early Spanish explorers, impressed by the mesa's lush greenness compared with the adjoining desert,

Cliff Palace, Mesa Verde National Park

Colorado Historical Society

called it, Mesa Verde, "Green Tableland." Indeed, gaining warmth off the desert and moisture off the nearby mountains, the roughly eighty-square-mile mesa is now, as in the past, carpeted with rich growths of piñon, juniper, Gambel oak, mountain mohagany, service berry, Fendler bush, and at higher elevations, Ponderosa pine, Douglas fir, and aspen.

The Mesa Verde and the Montelores Plateau, very hospitable lands by the standards of the Colorado Plateau, were the homeland of the Mesa Verde, or Northern San Juan, Anasazi cultural group.

The highest population density, as well as the apex of the Mesa Verde culture, was on the nearby Montelores Plateau, rather than on the now-famous Mesa Verde. Some, to date, unexcavated pueblos northwest of Cortez consisted of a thousand rooms or more, with perhaps as many as a hundred kivas in each pueblo. The Yellow Jacket ruin, for example, had an estimated 1,820 rooms, 166 kivas, a great kiva, four plazas, twenty towers, and housed upwards of three thousand people, a much larger population than even Chaco Canyon's enormous Pueblo Bonito. Meanwhile, as recently as 1990, another large ruin was discovered near Dove Creek, Colorado. Thus, the combined communities of the long-ago Montelores Plateau may have held a population of upwards of fifty thousand people, roughly three times the plateau's present population.

But it is to the legendary Mesa Verde to which people from around the world now trek, eager to see the amazing cliff dwellings built nearly a thousand years ago.

Ironically, these cliff dwellings, today protected within the boundaries of Mesa Verde National Park, were apparently built in response to a time of hardship that had befallen the Anasazi, hardship which was to eventually drive them from their homes in the Four Corners area. It was only during their final years there that the Anasazi built the cliff dwellings, as well as many of their most impressive—and baffling—free-standing pueblos.

Mesa Verde spreads like an enormous hand, with the palm toward the north, the fingers stretching south toward the desert. These "fingers" are formed by several canyons, cut into the heights of the mesa over millions of years. Each is lined with towering cliffs of sandstone and shale, deposited here ages ago when the Mesa Verde region was the eastern shore of a sea that covered much of Utah.

The first evidence of the Basketmaker Anasazi at Mesa Verde dates from about 550 A.D. By 1100 A.D., two hundred years later than the Chacoans, the Mesa Verdeans were in the Great Pueblo period.

The population of the Mesa Verde at its height was about five thousand people. Originally, the Mesa Verdeans lived in pueblos scattered across the mesa top. Although significantly smaller than the largest Chaco pueblos and of less refined construction, the Mesa Verde pueblos, such as Far View House, nonetheless were up to four-stories high and were beautiful and awe-inspiring in their own right. Among other of the Mesa Verde Anasazi accomplishments during the Great, or Classic, Pueblo era was the creation of elegant pottery, consisting of intricate geometric designs of black on gray.

But abruptly about 1150 A.D., about the same time that the Chacoans were abandoning their desert cities, at least some of the Mesa Verdeans moved under the overhangs of the nearby cliff faces and began to build cliff dwellings. The reason why is unknown. It may have been defensive; yet, archeologists have found little evidence of an invading people, and although the remains of some murdered Anasazi have been found on the Montelores Plateau, there is little other evidence of warfare. Perhaps the cliff dwellings indicated nothing more sinister than a need to conserve wood during a time of shortages, since many of the cliff structures, sheltered by overhanging rock, needed no roofs.

Whatever the reason, the Mesa Verde cliff dwellings fitted hand-in-glove into the protective sandstone overhangs. Multi-story dwellings were built toward the back of the pueblos; underground kivas, with plaza areas on top, rested toward the front. Cliff Palace, the largest cliff dwelling, had 217 rooms, 23 kivas, and housed approximately 250 people.

Why the Exodus?

But the Anasazi's attempt at adapting to adversity was not enough. Chaco Canyon was abandoned early, by 1150 A.D. By 1300 A.D. Mesa Verde stood empty, although at least some Mesa Verde Anasazi lived among the abandoned cities of Chaco Canyon for a time. Finally, even the diligent Kayenta Anasazi could persevere no longer and left Tsegi Canyon.

There have been many theories about what happened: drought, the spread of desertification triggered by agriculture-caused erosion, soil depletion, invading peoples, radical climate change, internal feuding, depletion of wood supplies for heating, cooking, and construction, overpopulation and/or environmental degradation caused by overpopulation, or epidemics spread along trading routes or triggered by malnutrition.

Dr. Linda S. Cordell, an archeologist and professor of anthropology at the University of New Mexico and a leading authority on the Anasazi, believes that there is no simple answer, that the reasons behind abandonment of any population center are complex, that a combination of some or all of the above factors may have woven into an intricate web of conditions which eventually caused the Anasazi to move on.

Cordell also focuses on another fact: While the abandonment of cities by Europeans rarely occurred, abandonment of major population centers throughout the Americas was commonplace. In fact, only rarely were population centers in the Southwest occupied for more than a few generations. Among the Anasazi, it was the norm to abandon an area, probably when resources became strained by a growing population, by climate changes, or when too many years of cultivation negatively impacted the soil and decreased crop yields. The Anasazi occasionally reoccupied an area one or two centuries later, perhaps after the land had a chance to heal itself or weather conditions had improved.

Dr. Kenneth Peterson, meanwhile, a paleoclimatologist recently involved in extensive

Sun Temple, Mesa Verde National Park

Colorado Historical Society

excavations near Dolores, Colorado, where the U.S. Bureau of Reclamation's McPhee Dam was about to flood extensive Anasazi sites, advances another theory. Based on information gained during that dig, Peterson maintains that drought, combined with colder weather, brought an end to the Anasazi in the Four Corners area.

From 600 A.D. to 750 A.D., the weather was warm and damp—nearly optimum—and the Anasazi culture thrived. About 750 A.D. a drought hit, albeit moderated by fairly heavy late-summer monsoons, and the Anasazi adapted by moving their fields to higher, damper elevations, such as Mesa Verde. By 1000 A.D. the climate again turned damp with continued moderate temperatures, and the Anasazi expanded their farm belt to include elevations down to 5,200 feet—to the depths of the San Juan Basin—an area nearly twice as extensive as that farmed in the region today. Soon, the Anasazi culture reached its zenith.

But then, beginning about 1150 A.D., came a new drought, compounded by a lack of critical summer rain. The Chacoan cities, at low altitudes in the heart of the San Juan Basin, succumbed fairly quickly, and then by 1200 A.D., the calamitous drought was compounded by drops in average annual temperatures. This prevented the Anasazi from cultivating crops in higher elevations, as they had in the previous drought. Meanwhile, their population had mushroomed. Even had high-altitude cultivation been possible, the lands of the Four Corners area might still have not provided adequate food without the use of low-altitude lands as well. The Anasazi were forced to leave.

Yet, during their last years in the Four Corners area, it seems they tried every conceivable way to remain.

Upon the Mesa Verde and on the Montelores Plateau, they built enormous pueblos apparently solely as ceremonial centers, perhaps in a religious attempt to seek modification of the adversity that was about to overcome them. Among these was Sun Temple at Mesa Verde and Sand Canyon Pueblo near Cortez.

Sand Canyon, built about 1240 A.D., consisted of roughly 350 rooms, with a four-to-one ratio of kivas to conventional rooms, unusually high, since the norm was about one kiva to every twelve rooms. These were developed around a central plaza so that the entire pueblo sprawled over an area about the size of three square city blocks. Yet, evidence indicates that this structure, which must have greatly taxed the resources of the Anasazi at a time when they were already severely stressed, was probably used only for ritual purposes.

But it was all in vain. Sand Canyon Pueblo was used for only about sixty years, and then the Anasazi left the San Juan forever.

The evacuation was gradual, a slow withdrawal over many years, until by 1300 A.D., all of the Anasazi were gone, the reason why they never returned as great a mystery as why they originally left.

Wupatki Ruin, Wupatki National Monument

Arizona Historical Society

The Sinagua

During the winter of 1064-1065 A.D., a volcano erupted near today's city of Flagstaff, Arizona, spewing accumulations of ash and cinder across eight hundred square miles of the surrounding Wupatki Basin. A farming people, like the Anasazi originating out of the Desert Archaic culture, the Sinagua had lived in the area for at least five hundred years but fled as their fields of corn, beans, and squash, as well as their pithouse homes, were destroyed by the onslaught.

Finally, about 1100 A.D., the Sinagua (Spanish for "Without Water") returned to discover fortune born of misfortune.

The thick accumulation of ash and cinder not only retained the region's marginal precipitation, both in the surface soil and in ground water, but it slightly lengthening the growing season by warming the soil. This, combined with a period of slightly damper weather, made Wupatki Basin nearly ideal for farming. The Sinagua were rapidly joined by people of other nearby, closely related cultures, the Hohokam and Mogollon from the central mountain and desert regions of Arizona to the south of the Colorado Plateau; the Cohonina from the northwest, between the Colorado and Little Colorado rivers along the South Rim of the Grand Canyon; and the Kayenta Anasazi, from near the Arizona-Utah border. Soon, dozens of villages proliferated at what is now Wupatki National Monument, and later, at what is now nearby Walnut Canyon National Monument.

The various cultures quickly blended into an amalgam, a colorful, thriving hybrid Sinaguan culture.

Multi-story pueblos, similar to those of the Anasazi, were constructed at Wupatki (a Hopi term which has been variously translated to mean "Great Rain Cloud Ruin," "Tall House," or "Red Ruins in Black Cinder"). A round ball court, a tradition originating in Central America and brought to northern Arizona by the Hohokam, was built, as was a round amphitheater, probably used for ceremonial or religious purposes. Kivas of many shapes, sizes, and variations—round above-ground kivas, square below-ground kivas, and round below-ground kivas—were also built. Meanwhile, the Sinagua made elaborate turquoise ornaments. And unlike the Anasazi, who buried their dead in a fetal position, the Sinagua partially cremated and then buried their dead with legs extended.

As the population of Wupatki grew, the overflow moved into nearby Walnut Canyon, where over three hundred cliff dwelling-type rooms were built into limestone ledges along the canyon walls.

But by 1225 A.D., the Sinagua had abandoned Wupatki Basin for reasons which are not entirely clear. Archeologists believe that soil depletion, combined with a sustained drought, perhaps compounded by the blowing-away of much of the once-protective ash, may have caused the dispersal.

Like the towns of the Anasazi, the villages of the Sinagua amalgam ultimately rested empty and silent.

Fremont Rock Art

Capitol Reef National Park

The Fremont

They were certainly here long ago, living in the canyons of the Colorado Plateau, drawing figures on sandstone walls, hunting animals in the desert and mountains. Yet, beyond a few simple facts gleaned from the ruins and relics of their lifeway, little is known. They were the mystery people of the Colorado Plateau, their history a baffling conundrum that has perplexed archeologists as to their genesis and their eventual fate.

The Fremont (named in modern times after southern Utah's Fremont River) lived north and west of the Colorado River, spreading throughout northwestern Colorado, Utah, and into Nevada at about the same time that the Anasazi were spreading throughout the Four Corners area. They lived only as far south as the Waterpocket Fold and Fremont River regions of what is now Capitol Reef National Park in south, central Utah.

Archeologists remain baffled as to their origins. Did they evolve out of the Desert Archaic culture, as did the Anasazi? Were they merely a splinter group of the Anasazi, living a different lifeway? Or, since they seemed to share many of the same cultural traits, such as wearing moccasins rather than sandals as did the Anasazi, were they Plains Indians who had found their way into Utah from eastern Colorado and Wyoming? At present, the theory that they evolved from the Desert Archaic culture enjoys the broadest acceptance.

Before 500 A.D. the Fremont, like the Anasazi, lived in pithouses and cultivated crops nearby, after having evolved from a strictly hunting-gathering culture. However, they probably depended upon agriculture less and on hunting more than did the Anasazi. Meanwhile, their buildings never took on the grandeur of those of the Anasazi. They continued to live in pithouses, while the surface structures that they did build remained small and comparatively few in number, and they built no kivas. They did construct small granaries and storage pits, and they made lovely pottery, gray in its original color, but decorated with strips of clay molded into various animal shapes or painted with geometric designs after firing. They also made elaborate clay and wood figurines, probably of religious significance, sometimes in pairs, male and female, or single figures representing a pregnant woman, or figures with human-like bodies and bird-like heads.

And they created hauntingly beautiful rock art on desert cliff faces, at Dinosaur National Monument and Canyonlands, Capitol Reef, and Arches national parks and elsewhere, depicting not only wildlife, but human figures, some of them drawn to appear to be carrying likenesses of human heads. (Some rock art in these regions, such as the spectacular Great Gallery in Canyonlands National Park, predates even the Fremont people by several thousand years.)

But the final mystery of the Fremont is what became of them after they, like the Anasazi, left the isolated canyons of Utah by about 1300 A.D.

They may have cast off the burden of their stone dwelling places and farms and returned to a strictly hunting-gathering culture, wandering the desert and mountains of Utah and Colorado, perhaps the ancestors of today's Ute and/or Southern Paiute people. Perhaps they returned to the Great Plains region of the central

United States to hunt buffalo and live a nomadic lifeway. Or perhaps they moved southward, as did the Anasazi, although little evidence of such a migration has been found.

What became of them is as enigmatic as the strange rock-art figures that they left behind to stare blindly, disconcertingly down into the eyes of present-day visitors to the Colorado Plateau.

Part Two
Historical Times

Pueblo Woman
Colorado Historical Society

Woman Grinding Corn, Cochiti Pueblo, New Mexico
Colorado Historical Society

The Pueblos

When the Anasazi left the Four Corners area, it was not the end of them or their way of life, merely a transition period, a time when they moved on into a new era upon the Colorado Plateau and across much of the Southwest.

The Anasazi were the ancestors of those known collectively today as the Pueblo people*, specifically the Hopis of northeastern Arizona, the Zuñis to the west of Albuquerque, New Mexico, and the Rio Grande Pueblo people, along the Rio Grande Valley of north, central New Mexico just beyond the southeastern edge of the Colorado Plateau. The Pueblo villages that now dot the plateaus and river valleys of northern New Mexico and northern Arizona are manifestations of the living continuum of the Anasazi tradition. Although the people of the various Pueblo villages of the present often speak different languages, as probably did their Anasazi ancestors, they share the same basic cultural traits and the same general Anasazi ancestry.

From the Mesa Verde, Chaco Canyon, and Kayenta regions, the Anasazi dispersed southeast, south, and southwest to places, in most cases, already inhabited by others of their numbers. The present-day Hopi village of Oraibi, for example, existed in 1100 A.D., a time during which the Anasazi still lived at Kayenta, Mesa Verde, and Chaco Canyon. Oraibi may have existed in some form a thousand years before that.

The places to which specific cultural groups moved, however, remains basically an unsolved puzzle. Archeologists have examined archeological clues and anthropologists have studied migration legends of modern-day Pueblo people, largely in vain, in order to find proof of which Anasazi cultural group went where during the dispersal.

What archeologists do know is that, as the Anasazi left their Four Corners-area homes, there were significant increases in the populations of many already established pueblo communities. Probably, since the Anasazi people dispersed a few at a time—perhaps a few individuals or even an entire clan group at once—rather than by community-wide evacuations, they scattered widely, going to live in or near established communities where they already had friends or family.

The Hopi people believe that they are variously the descendants of the Kayenta and Sinagua Anasazi, perhaps confirmed in part by present-day square-shaped Hopi kivas, or kihus, although some Hopi verbal tradition also states that they are descended from the Mesa Verde Anasazi. Some of the Chacoans, meanwhile, may have moved to present-day Acoma, seventy-five miles south of Chaco Canyon and occupied nearly as long ago as Oraibi, or to Zuñi. The largest surviving pueblo in the Southwest, Zuñi boasts elaborate stonework similar to that at Chaco.

Archeologists call this period, from about 1300 A.D. to 1600 A.D., the Regressive, or Renaissance, Pueblo era. The Anasazi culture did not eclipse or slip into obscurity during that era. In fact, of all of the Anasazi cultural divisions, only the Chaco culture declined, and at the time of Coronado's expedition of 1540, the Spaniards found roughly one hundred inhabited Pueblo villages, mostly along the Rio Grande. They also found evidence

(*When capitalized, Pueblo refers to the people; uncapitalized it refers to their pueblo homes and villages.)

of literally hundreds of other previously inhabited communities.

In contrast, today there are only about thirty occupied Pueblo villages. There are the Hopi villages of Walpi, Hano, Sitchumovi, Shungopovi, Shipaulovi, Mishongnovi, Oraibi, Moencopi, Hotevilla, Bacabi, and Kykotsmovi, with a combined population of about seven thousand people as of 1980. There are the northern New Mexico villages of Zuñi, forty miles southwest of Gallup, New Mexico, and Acoma and Laguna, west of Albuquerque, New Mexico, with a combined population of about thirteen thousand people; and there are the Rio Grande-area villages of Zía, Santo Domingo, Santa Ana, San Felipe, Cóchiti, Taos, Jémez, Picuris, Sandía, Isleta, San Juan, Santa Clara, San Ildefonso, Tesuque, and Nambé, with a combined population of roughly twenty-six thousand people as of the 1980 census.

The Conquest

When the Spanish *Conquistadores* moved north from Mexico, they undoubtedly represented a frightening sight to the indigenous people of the Southwest. They wore strange metal armor, carried guns—which they took delight in discharging for the sole purpose of frightening the local populace—and rode horses, animals long extinct in the Americas and never before seen by the indigenous people.

The first Pueblo village seen by Europeans was in 1539, when Fray Marcos de Niza, an Italian in service of Spain, guided by a Moor by a the name of Estaban, led an expedition in search of the legendary Seven Cities of Cíbola, mythical cities of gold that had been part of Spanish lore since the ninth century. Estaban was killed by the people of the Zuñi pueblo, and de Niza, waiting in view of the pueblo and hearing of the death, fled back to Mexico, nonetheless convinced that he had seen one of the legendary cities.

De Niza was followed by the Coronado expedition of the following year, during which Coronado and his men massacred the entire pueblo village of Tiguex on the Rio Grande. The colonizing mission of Juan de Oñata, meanwhile, arrived in 1598, and in 1610 Santa Fe was founded. Thus began what is known as the Historic Pueblo era. Stretching from 1600 to the present, much of that era has been a time of profound suffering for the Pueblo people.

Many were sold into slavery, while the Spanish confiscated crops, raped, pillaged, pastured their horses in Pueblo fields, and exacted exorbitant duties, usually in the form of food, since the Spaniards were often unable to fend adequately for themselves in the rugged land to which they had moved. At times the duties became so unreasonable that the Pueblos themselves starved.

The Spaniards also attempted to destroy the Pueblo religion, which was not only the center of spiritual life, it also comprised a complicated set of ceremonies, traditions, and beliefs guiding all aspects of Pueblo government, social life, crop planting, and harvesting. Those Pueblo people who resisted the invasion were flogged, hanged, or sometimes burned alive. At Acoma pueblo, which unsuccessfully withstood a prolonged

Pueblo Child, Isleta Pueblo, New Mexico

Colorado Historical Society

siege in defiance of the Spaniards, hundreds died resisting the Spanish. After the conquest, each surviving warrior had a foot hacked off by the Spaniards to thwart further resistance.

In addition to deliberate cruelty, the Spaniards inadvertently introduced measles, smallpox, and other European diseases, to which the Pueblos and other Native Americans had no natural immunity. The results were catastrophic. Many Native American populations have not recovered from the resulting deaths to this day. Largely as a result of epidemics, the Pueblo people, confined together in towns and therefore particularly vulnerable to disease, declined so radically in population that by 1700 only eighteen of the original one hundred pueblo villages seen in 1540 remained.

Finally, in 1680, after a previous unsuccessful uprising in 1642, the Pueblos, with the help of the Apaches, revolted and drove the Spaniards out. Led by Popé of the San Juan Pueblo, the revolt spread to all of the Pueblo villages, even to the remote Hopi mesas of northern Arizona, the only time in recorded history that the many autonomous villages of the Pueblos acted in unison.

Some four hundred Spanish settlers and eighteen priests were killed by the enraged Pueblos, the rest were allowed to flee south along the Rio Grande. But the Pueblos paid dearly to gain their freedom, losing 350 people, 47 of them captured and executed by the Spaniards before the Spaniards fled.

Afterwards, the Pueblos held the Spaniards at bay for twelve years. In 1692, however, Don Diego de Vargas reconquered the New Mexico Pueblos. The Arizona pueblos were different. The Hopis (from the Hopi term, *Hopituh Shi-nu-mu*, meaning "The Peaceful People") had historically been the most nonviolent of all the Pueblos, Nonetheless, they firmly resisted reoccupation and were never reconquered.

The price of the Pueblos' brief taste of freedom was high. At the Tano Pueblo in the Galisteo Basin south of Santa Fe, for example, eighty-one Pueblo people were executed for resisting the Spaniards' return. Six hundred others from various villages were sold into slavery in the West Indies, never to see their homes, families, or beloved Southwest again.

For some of the Pueblo people, Spanish domination became intolerable. Many fled their Rio Grande-area homes to live elsewhere. In 1696, the Jémez Pueblo unsuccessfully revolted and was ultimately abandoned for a time, as its people fled to live among the Navajos. In fact, to this day Navajos of the Coyote Pass clan trace much of their ancestry to Jémez. Other residents of Rio Grande-area pueblos, meanwhile, were sheltered by the Hopis in Arizona and were invited to establish their own village there, today's village of Hano.

And during the four hundred years since the Spanish reconquest, the Pueblos' beloved Southwest has continued to remain occupied, first by Spain until 1820, then Mexico until 1835, and finally, by the United States.

The Ways of the Ancients

While some things were lost under the onslaught, the

Pueblo people managed to retain the essence—the core—of Pueblo life. To do so, however, sometimes meant hardship and suffering. In 1906, for example, the U.S. Army forcefully removed Hopi children from their homes and took them to a boarding school at Keams Canyon, Arizona, where they were forbidden to speak the Hopi language or to practice their native religion. This was all part of what was then an official government policy of trying to assimilate, sometimes through force, Native Americans into mainstream society. By definition, the goal of this policy was the destruction of indigenous cultures.

Beyond that, while the Pueblo people were for the most part permitted to remain in their historic pueblo villages, reservations were established around the villages which were without exception much smaller than the indigenous lands the people had historically used. The Hopi reservation, for example, a comparatively small area of land, is completely surrounded by the Navajo reservation. Population growth, particularly among the Navajos, and land-use conflicts between the two people, compounded by the intrusion of major energy development, has led to the festering problems of the so-called Navajo-Hopi land dispute. Violence threatened on several occasions in recent years when the U.S. government tried to implement a policy of removing Navajos from Hopi lands, a policy certainly opposed by the Navajo nation and not entirely supported by the Hopis.

In the face of such assaults, however, many Pueblo traditions and customs have persevered to contribute a kaleidoscope of color and beauty to life in the Southwest.

The best way to appreciate the Pueblo tradition is to gaze upon the beauty of age-old pueblos and to observe a way of life with which the Anasazi and their descendants have persevered, if not always thrived. (Because of too many intrusions on the Pueblos' privacy, visitors are unwelcome in some villages and in some others may enter only under special conditions.)

In the pueblos, often large, sprawling complexes the color of the desert earth, ladders still protrude from kivas and children run through the complicated maze of streets as must have generations of children before them. Often, at the pueblos along the Rio Grande and in the shadow of Mount Taylor to the west of Albuquerque, churches built by the conquering Spaniards protrude from the depths of the villages. However, Spanish missions built among the Hopi villages were demolished by the Hopis in the wake of the Pueblo Revolt and were never permitted to be rebuilt.

And in ancient tradition, there are the fields which provide much of the food for the pueblos.

In the Rio Grande valley, fields are cultivated along the fertile bottomlands, where it is easy to divert water for irrigation. However, on the sunbaked Hopi mesas of northern Arizona, most of the fields of corn, beans, squash, peach trees, and cotton are unirrigated, with the exception of those at Moenkopi, the western-most village. The only pueblo located off of the three Hopi mesas, it rests along the at least intermittent waters of Moenkopi Wash.

Walpi Pueblo, Arizona

Colorado Historical Society

Although not quite as dry as a true desert, such as the Mojave, on average only about twelve inches of moisture annually falls on the semi-arid Hopi mesas, the driest part of the Colorado Plateau. Yet, crops survive both because of the prudent use of water and, the Hopis would hasten to add, because of the Hopi peoples' meticulous adherence to religious tradition.

With the wisdom of ages spent on the Colorado Plateau, the Hopis—often using traditional digging sticks, as did their ancestors before them—plant their crops deeply, sometimes a foot or more into the sandy soil, sheltering seeds and roots from the drying winds of the Painted Desert. Other crops are planted on sometimes elaborately terraced and walled areas along the edges of the mesas. Rainwater running off the pueblo rooftops and streets finds its way onto the terraces below, while walls protect crops from the relentless wind. Stunted little peach trees and corn, meanwhile, grow in the alluvial plains at the base of the mesas, where both surface and underground runoff from the mesa tops eventually flow.

And other age-old customs survive.

Pueblo women still own all household property and usually the seeds for planting. Girl babies, meanwhile, are often preferred over boys by expectant parents, who look at them as essential to the perpetuation of the clan, several of which comprise each pueblo village. Clan membership is determined matrilineally, or through the female line, and a couple settles matrilocally, or with the wife's family.

Since a married couple adhering to the traditional ways often settles in the house owned by a woman's mother and her mother's mother before her, it is not uncommon for a woman to live her entire life in one house. In some cases, as at Zuñi, although the men do all of the farm work, the women own the resulting crops; however, it should be emphasized that in the highly communal villages of the Pueblo people, ownership does not imply the same connotations as it does in other economies. The men, meanwhile, as in the time of the Anasazi, do the weaving, often in the kivas. The kivas are owned by the men and are the center of religious ceremony, social activities, and craft work.

The beautiful pueblo villages, meanwhile, reflect a centuries-old building tradition. In many pueblos today, women do much of the stone work, leading archeologists to believe that the detailed stone work at Chaco Canyon may have been done, all or in part, by the Anasazi women.

The Age-Old Faith

Pueblo life is centered around religious observances with roots going back into the antiquity of the Colorado Plateau.

Religion dominates virtually every aspect of pueblo and family life. In fact, there is often no practical distinction between the secular and the religious. Village civic leadership and religious leadership are either one and the same, or secular leaders are strongly influenced by village religious elders. Elders gain increasing influence as they age and are freed from secular responsibilities, such as helping with the crops, in order to increasingly devote their time and energies to religious priorities.

As in the time of the Anasazi, solar astronomy plays an important role in predicting the solstices, the equinoxes, and other seasonal sacred occasions. A day rarely passes without an important religious observance, part of a complicated, interrelated web of ritual and ceremony closely integrated to the passing of the seasons. It is a religion so bewilderingly intricate that anthropologists who have studied it still have only a general understanding of it.

The Pueblos, as is universally the case with the indigenous people of the Colorado Plateau, believe that, rather than migrating from Asia via the Bering Strait, they climbed to the surface of this world from a world below. They also honor six sacred directions, north, east, south, and west, plus the upper world of the living, and the lower world of the dead.

The sun rises from his "house" in the east, journeys across the sky, lighting this world, then to set in his "house" in the west, and from there to travel back to the east, lighting the underworld while he moves. The point of original emergence, as exemplified by the *sipapu,* a symbolic hole at the bottom of every kiva, leads to the underworld from which the Pueblo people emerged during remote antiquity and to which the dead return within a few days of death. The two worlds are not considered to be spiritually separate but are part of a continuum, with reciprocity and communication between the two through the spirits of the dead, who can move easily from one to the other.

The Pueblos see the universe as being animate, with virtually everything in it having a spiritual essence. The natural, the supernatural, the living, the dead, man, animals, plants, the Earth, sun, moon, clouds, water, rocks, trees, even food, have a spiritual essence. All things are interrelated and mutually dependant. Most elements operate automatically, guided by the dynamics of the universe; however, humankind, by living properly, can positively influence events. Humankind can likewise communicate with the forces of nature and with the sun through various means, including prayer sticks, or *pahos,* small sticks with sacred eagle feathers attached, each carrying forth a message on the wind.

Therefore, the Pueblos believe that elaborate rituals help to keep the world in harmony, ceremonies which help to encourage the supernatural beings—the greatest divinity of all, as symbolized by the sun, and lesser divinities, the *Katchinas,* thought to be the spirits of the dead—to positively influence the forces of nature. (At Zuñi, Katchinas are known as *Shalako.*)

Katchinas were not always part of Pueblo religion. Katchina cults apparently began sometime between 1350 and 1540, during the Renaissance Pueblo era. The earliest known Katchina figures, in the form of rock art, are found in the vicinity of El Paso, Texas, while the Hopis and the Zuñis were apparently the first Pueblos to integrate them into their religions.

The Pueblos believe that Katchinas, or Shalako, are linked to the coming of rain, the growing of crops, and the general well-being of the pueblo villages. The

Hopi Weaver, 1901

Colorado Historical Society

Katchinas are kind, caring, compassionate beings, who reside in sacred lakes, streams, springs, or on mountain tops. When they come to dance—in fact Pueblo men dressed in Katchina costumes and masks and transformed through a religious miracle akin to Christian Sacramental wine becoming the blood of Christ—it is believed they cause the rains to fall, of particular importance in this harsh, dry land. The Katchina masks, worn by the Kachina dancers, have been handed down along family lines for countless generations, the Pueblos say, "since time began."

And, as in the lives of their Anasazi ancestors before them, the kiva is still the center of religious activity. In fact, the building and maintenance of a kiva are believed to be sacred acts, analogous to prayer.

The men of the village belong to particular kiva societies, with membership to a kiva often determined by heredity. As in the past, the kiva contains a firepit with a ventilation shaft, entrance usually via a ladder through the ceiling, and a sipapu in the floor. The kiva itself, recessed into the ground or built to create the illusion of being recessed into the ground, symbolizes the world below from which the Pueblo people emerged. To leave the kiva via the ladder is a symbolic reenactment of that emergence.

The various religious societies within a Pueblo each have specific responsibilities aimed at maintaining balance and order within the universe. The status of these all-male societies is based upon the importance of the ceremonies they perform. In the Hopi villages, for example, the Soyal Society performs one of the most important religious observances, the winter solstice ceremony, during which the sun, deep on the southern horizon, is guided into the beginning of its return journey to the north. Therefore, the Soyal holds perhaps the single greatest ceremonial responsibility. However, membership in such societies is looked upon not as a matter of prestige but as a matter of responsibility toward the well-being of the pueblo, part of a faith which has ritualized and structured life so as to keep the Pueblo people in harmony with the harsh, sometimes unforgiving land upon which they depend. Crop plantings, for example, are precisely determined by religious protocol so as to give plants the optimum amount of time to ripen before the killing frosts of the Colorado Plateau's early autumn.

Socially, the Pueblos foster a spirit of cooperation, sometimes making the interests of the individual ancillary to the collective good of the community. Perhaps this reflects centuries of living in a harsh land, where internal dissension might contribute to community unrest and a resulting bad harvest, even starvation. Nonetheless, while aggressive, assertive, or loud behavior is strongly condemned, the individual is deeply respected as a valuable part of the community.

Disputes, such as divorces, meanwhile, are governed by strict codes of behavior, which minimize disruption to both the family and the community. In most pueblos, for example, if a woman decides to divorce her husband, she simply places his belongings outside the house; he then returns, without protest, to the home of his mother. Nor does divorce carry any form of social stigma; the end of a marriage is treated philosophically, as part of the routine course of human life. Meanwhile, since the rearing of children is closely tied to the mother's ancestral home, which is filled with many aunts, uncles, and cousins—who are thought of in almost virtually the same light as mothers, fathers, brothers, and sisters—divorce lacks much of the shattering potential it has in small, nuclear families consisting solely of parents and children.

In addition, in such an environment, Pueblo children are showered with attention and guidance, perhaps contributing to such things as the fact that Hopi children frequently score far above the national average on intelligence tests.

And while the Anasazi embraced the beauty around them, as was reflected in their pottery, basketry, and weaving, so too do the Pueblo people of the present.

There is the distinctive, glossy, solid-black or orange pottery, almost instantly recognizable as coming from the Santa Clara Pueblo. There is the unique black-and-white Acoma pottery, a revival of many of the designs used by the Anasazi people. There are the brightly colored polychrome pots of the Hopis, incorporating vivid reds, oranges, and blacks, and often reflecting sacred symbols. And there are the playful clay figures of the Cóchiti Pueblo, including humorous, but affectionate, depictions of tourists or the famous and equally humorous "Storyteller," spinning yarns to a cluster of eagerly listening youngsters.

And there are baskets, intricately woven of native plant fibers, often yucca, a sacred plant to many Native Americans. Some such baskets are sold as craft items throughout the Southwest. Others still perform a functional purpose during day-to-day life within the pueblos.

And as in the time of the ancients, there is weaving, done by the Pueblo men.

Each year, beginning with the winter solstice, the Katchinas intermittently appear in the Hopi villages. Each appearance throughout the following months is of tremendous spiritual importance, meant to assure the Katchinas that the Hopi people are trying to live a pure and good life and are worthy of the Katchinas' efforts on their behalf. Finally, in late July, the Katchinas appear in the villages for the last times before returning to the heights of the San Francisco Peaks, some eighty miles to the southwest. There they will prepare to bring rain to the Hopis' crops during the rainy season of August and September.

It is during these final visits that an important and solemn ceremony is conducted, during which Hopi brides are presented to the Katchinas. For the ceremony, each bride wears a white cotton robe woven by her husband's uncles, part of a tradition going back generations among the Hopis.

Each bride also wears the same robe when she ceremonially presents her first-born child to the sun, at dawn twenty days after the child's birth. Finally, when the woman dies, she is buried in another white robe, which she held in her arms on the day she was married.

Thus, resolutely, beautifully, a centuries-old way of life endures.

Navajo Men, Circa 1920

William M. Pennington, Colorado Historical Society

The Navajos

A Navajo woman weaving a blanket or a Navajo man riding a horse across a desert sanddune are images virtually symbolic of the American Southwest. While the towering buttes of Left Mitten, Right Mitten, or Merrick Butte in Monument Valley immediately come to mind at the mention of the Painted Desert, a Navajo herding sheep nearby is almost invariably part of that picture.

Yet, compared with the Pueblo people who have lived on the Colorado Plateau for thousands of years, the Navajo are relative newcomers.

The earliest conclusively proven Navajo settlement, found in New Mexico's Gobernador Canyon, dates from about 1541 A.D., although the remains of what may have been Navajo homes, dating from before 1000 A.D., have also been found in western Colorado. Nonetheless, many archeologists believe the Navajos weren't in the Southwest before 1300 A.D. There is some possibility that the first straggling groups of Navajos and other Apaches arriving in the region may have played some part in the departure of the Anasazi; however, the Anasazi may have instead been harassed by Shoshonean-speaking people, the Utes or Paiutes, or as stated earlier, may have departed the area for reasons which had little to do with an encroaching people.

All that is known with certainty is that some time during antiquity, for reasons which will probably never be known, people from western Canada began to work their way southward in small bands, perhaps along the eastern foothills of the Rocky Mountains, perhaps through western Colorado or eastern Utah, perhaps through the Great Basin region of Nevada and western

Utah, or more probably, straggling in along several different routes over a period of several generations, a fact partially confirmed by Navajo myths and verbal tradition. These early Athabascan-speaking people were the ancestors of today's Navajo and Apache people, who to this day can understand at least some of the language of the Sekani people of Canada.

Early Navajos on the Colorado Plateau built forked-stick *hogans*, round dwellings consisting of wooden poles leaned together at the peak and then plastered over with grass, sticks, and mud—structures very similar to the pole dwellings, covered with branches and leaves, of the Canadian Athabascans.

From lush Canadian coastal areas, the migrating Athabascans, or at least their descendants, slowly found their way onto the arid, rugged expanses of the Colorado Plateau. When they first arrived, they were exclusively hunter-gathers but that was soon to change.

Strangers of the Fields

The Tewa Pueblo people originally named the newcomers, *Apachu*, meaning "strangers" or "enemies." But one group of Apaches they referred to differently. They called them the *Apachu de Nabahu*, "Strangers of the Cultivated Fields." At least some of the Apaches, probably those living in or near the Rio Grande Valley—"The Land of the Corn Growers"—had learned to farm, most likely from the Pueblo people. In fact, the adaptable Navajos learned more than farming from the Pueblos. Many imitated the Pueblos' urban lifeway by sometimes grouping their hogans together in communities of fifty or more, with fields nearby. Sometimes hogan communities and pueblos stood side-by-side. The Navajos most likely also learned to weave from the Pueblos, probably when the Navajos sheltered Pueblo refugees in the wake of the Pueblo Revolt.

The Navajos first officially began to be recognized as a distinctive people in 1626 when Fray Zarata Salmeron referred to them as being separate from other Apaches, and in 1630 when Fray Alonso de Benavides, while writing to Spain, spoke of the distinction between them and other Apaches. Using the Spanish spelling for the Tewa term he had heard, or thought he had heard, Benavides wrote of the *Apachu de Navajo*, thus the term "Navajo" was launched.

The Navajos nonetheless think of themselves not as Navajos, but as the *Diné*, "The People," or "The Earth Surface People," a name based on their belief that long ago, rising through a hole somewhere deep in the San Juan Mountains, their gods found a way to the surface of this world from a world below, then to create the Diné.

But they were not to remain sedentary farmers.

In 1598 Don Juan de Õnate headed a colonizing mission into the northern Rio Grande Valley from Mexico. In addition to 130 troops, the contingent consisted of priests, families, and retainers to bring the number of settlers to four hundred. But perhaps just as important, a great cloud of dust rose skyward as the assembly traveled along, for Õnate also brought domestic animals into the Southwest.

Into a world that had had no domestic animals except dogs and turkeys came 1,100 cattle, 4,000 sheep for wool and mutton, 1,000 goats, 150 colts, and 150 mares. These animals were supposedly reserved for the exclusive use of the Spaniards; however, after the Pueblo Revolt of 1680, the animals slipped into the possession of the indigenous people. The Pueblos, particularly those along the Rio Grande, began to tend cattle, sheep, and goats along with crops. Meanwhile, the Navajos embarked on a whole new way of life.

They became shepherds, but they and other Apaches also became horsemen, loving horses for the freedom and mobility the animals gave them. They rapidly put aside any inclination to live in communities. Horses meant that they could freely wander the Southwest. More, the Navajos soon discovered that the ownership of herd animals helped assure that the Diné could roam with little threat of hunger.

Soon, most Navajos were again living an at least semi-nomadic lifeway, following a pattern established by the grazing of their herds. Many moved into the foothills of the towering San Juans or into the depths of the desert mountain ranges in summer to graze their animals, returning to the warmer lower regions in winter. In summer, if they built a dwelling at all, it was simply a branch-and-stick-covered square shelter with no walls—what the Spaniards called a "ramada"—to shade them from the heat of the sun. In winter they lived in hogans, circular structures built of stone and mud and later, especially after the arrival of steel tools to cut and shape the wood, out of wood beams arranged hexagonally, caulked with mud, and roofed with dirt.

Nonetheless, the Navajos did not abandon the cultivation of crops. Some grew crops near summer grazing areas, while those who adhered to more localized patterns of grazing for their animals cultivated crops near hogans in which they lived year around.

But horses also brought other changes.

Although made officially illegal by royal Spanish decree in 1532, slavery was an accepted institution throughout Spanish territories in the New World. This was due in part to the tremendous amount of work to be done to accomplish the Spaniards' goal of building a new empire, in part because of the shortage of people to do that work. Although the Pueblos had represented an ideal source of slaves, as the Spanish empire expanded, even more people were needed to build cities and to work the enormous ranches of New Mexico and Mexico and the silver mines of Mexico.

Very soon Navajos and Utes of the Colorado Plateau; Comanches, a hunting-gathering, Shoshonean-speaking people of Colorado's and New Mexico's Great Plains region; and Apaches of southern New Mexico and southern Arizona discovered a tremendous opportunity. By the 1690s, using horses which allowed them to rapidly travel significant distances and to expeditiously ride into and out of various settlements, they were kidnapping at will. Annually, the horse-riding raiders gathered together the people they had captured and took them to Taos, New Mexico, to be sold as slaves, while the Spaniards rounded up every horse they could spare—the payment the horsemen coveted.

The Navajos also rapidly discovered that raids on other Native American communities and on Spanish ranches throughout New Mexico and northern Mexico gave them the opportunity to significantly expand the size of their herds. Sheep, in particular, were taken by the hundreds, horses at every opportunity. After weeks of raiding, the Navajos not uncommonly returned to the depths of the desert with thousands of animals, although it should be remembered that the Navajos were often similarly the victim of raids.

Yet, the isolated, uncharted miles of their vast homeland helped protect them from reprisals by the Spaniards. If pursued after a raid, the Navajos simply disappeared into their enormous domain. Early Spanish explorers had despaired at the idea of entering those rugged, nearly impassable lands and had simply labeled them, *tierra incognito*, "lands unknown," on their maps and had passed them by. The Navajos, confident that no one would follow them into the maze of canyons and high plateaus that represented their homeland, raided with near impunity.

Therefore, horses not only gave the Navajos, Apaches, Utes, and other indigenous peoples a new way of life, thanks to the Spaniards nearly insatiable appetite for slaves, horses also helped bring anarchy to the Southwest—anarchy lasting nearly two hundred years before it was brought to a swift and terrible conclusion by the United States.

The Long Walk

During the early 1860s, the U.S. government

Navajo, "Strong Man," Circa 1920

William M. Pennington, Colorado Historical Society

determined that the Navajo marauders must be subdued, both to stop their incessant raiding and to remove them from valuable lands which would soon be desired by white settlers.

Headed by explorer and Indian agent Col. Kit Carson, the New Mexico Volunteers had been mustered during the Civil War to help prevent pro-Confederate Arizona and Texas from giving aid to the Confederacy. The all-civilian regiment was also pressed into duty to subdue the Navajos, as well as the Mescalero and Jicarilla Apaches of New Mexico's eastern plains.

Carson, whom the Navajos called "Red Shirt," knew that military force brought directly to bear against the Navajos would be useless. Rather than fight, they would simply fade into the remote back country until danger passed, a problem compounded by a lack of cohesive leadership among the highly migratory people. The Navajos traveled in family groups or in dozens of loosely organized bands. While an agreement might be reached with one band to halt its raiding, others would merely continue.

Therefore, Carson and his troops, in addition to killing every male Navajo they came across, set about methodically starving the Navajos into submission.

They entered known Navajo strongholds throughout the Colorado Plateau region, burning fields, destroying orchards, and either killing or taking Navajo livestock. Carson and his men, for example, spent seven days burning large fields of corn and wheat near Canyon de Chelly, Arizona. In addition, Carson placed a bounty on Navajo livestock captured by other indigenous people,

an opportunity taken advantage of, in particular, by the Utes. Carson was also willing to look the other way if citizens of the New Mexico and Arizona territories sold captured Navajos to Mexican slavers—this even though the U.S. was even then fighting a war against slavery.

Finally, by the spring of 1864, with most of the Navajos weakened by starvation, they began to slowly straggle in out of the desert to surrender, although certainly many escaped into the most remote regions of Navajo country: the isolated lands near Navajo Mountain in Utah near the Arizona border, into the depths of the Grand Canyon, or across the San Juan River into the formidable canyons of southern Utah. Those who surrendered were herded into corrals and detained at Fort Wingate, near Grants, New Mexico, or at Fort Defiance, Arizona, on the Arizona-New Mexico border southeast of Canyon de Chelly.

From here began what the Navajos consider to be one of the most infamous events in U.S. history, the "Long Walk."

In several large groups totaling six thousand people, the Navajos were herded more than three hundred miles across the desert to Fort Sumner in extreme southeastern New Mexico. Only the very old, the infirm, or the very young were allowed to ride in wagons. The rest had to walk. Many already weakened by hunger died along the way.

But the ultimate horror for the Navajos was that they were being driven beyond the boundaries of *Diné Bikéyah*, the sacred Navajo homeland.

Long ago, when the Navajo gods climbed to the

surface of this world from the world below, they carried with them earth taken from subterranean mountains of the previous world. This they piled at the four points of the compass, north, east, south, and west, respectively, to create the sacred mountains marking the outer edges of Diné Bikéyah.

Thus, at the southern edge of the La Plata range of the San Juan Mountains, towers the thirteen-thousand-foot heights of Hesperus Peak, *Dibé Nitsaa*, the northern-most boundary of Diné Bikéyah. Meanwhile, along the eastern edge of the San Luis Valley in south, central Colorado, towers the sacred heights of Mount Blanca, or *Sis Najiní*. Jutting fourteen thousand feet into the Colorado sky, it represents the eastern-most edge of Diné Bikéyah. Far to the south, along the southern edge of the San Juan Basin, towers Mount Taylor; the Navajos call it, *Dsoodził*. Its volcanic heights jut 11,389 feet from the flatness of the New Mexico desert to form the southern boundary of Diné Bikéyah, while nearly three hundred miles due west of Mount Taylor, near Flagstaff, Arizona, rises the western-most sacred mountain, *Doo'k ó oosłiid*, the San Francisco Peaks. With heights rising to over ten thousand feet, those peaks mark the western boundary of Diné Bikéyah.

As the Navajo were marched to Fort Sumner, they realized that they were being forced to go beyond the boundaries, formed by the sacred mountains, of their homeland. They believed that the sacred songs, such as the Blessingway, perhaps the oldest and undoubtedly the most important of all Navajo religious ceremonies, would no longer be effective. They felt disenfranchised not only from their homeland but from their gods.

Finally, after a journey of weeks, the Navajos were herded into Fort Sumner, a prison camp beside the Little Pecos River. Here, at Bosque Redondo (Spanish for "Round Grove") over seven thousand Navajos and four hundred Mescalero Apaches were held prisoner for nearly five years. Hundreds died from malnutrition, disease, heat, and cold.

Eventually, after signing the Treaty of 1868, in which they agreed to never fight again, the Navajos were allowed to return home to live on a newly created reservation in their beloved redrock country of northeastern Arizona, northwestern New Mexico, and southeastern Utah.

"When we saw the top of the (southern sacred) mountain from Albuquerque," recalled one Navajo leader of the return from Bosque Redondo, "we wondered if it was our mountain, and we felt like talking to the ground, we loved it so, and some of the old men and women cried with joy...."

The New Diné Bikéyah

Although the largest reservation in the United States, now at about 16.5 million acres, the Navajo reservation to which the Diné returned was much smaller than Diné Bikéyah. Many could not in fact return to their homes, particularly in eastern Diné Bikéyah, near the Rio Grande in north, central New Mexico or in southwestern Colorado.

And when the Navajos returned home, it was to

more years of suffering. Their horses were gone, their herd animals were dead or had been stolen, their fields were destroyed, and they lacked seeds with which to plant new crops. For a time the U.S. government, itself heavily burdened by the debt of the Civil War, was to provide them with provisions and later with new herd animals, but often the provisions did not arrive. The new livestock, meanwhile, were months in coming. Complete destitution, even starvation, confronted the Diné. Sometimes they were reduced to eating rats and whatever wild plants they could find.

U.S. officials hoped that ultimately the Navajos would return to the reservation and support themselves solely by farming and animal husbandry in the tradition of the yeoman farmer, an idea probably formulated by those who had never seen the arid expanses of the Colorado Plateau.

Some years later, in the 1870s, an Indian agent working on the Navajo reservation wrote in a report to Washington, D.C., "The reservation embraces about ten thousand square-miles of the most worthless land that ever laid outdoors.... The country is almost entirely rock. An Illinois or Iowa or Kansas farmer would laugh to scorn the assertion that you could raise anything there. However, seventeen thousand Indians manage to extract their living from it without government aid. If they were not the best Indians on the continent, they would not do it...."

But somehow, the Navajos survived.

In 1869 fourteen thousand sheep and one thousand goats finally arrived—two animals for every man,

woman, and child. Wrote the military commandant who distributed the animals to the Navajos, "I have never seen such anxiety and gratitude."

The Navajos often cared for and nurtured their new livestock while going hungry themselves, postponing butchering the animals so that the animals could multiply. All the Navajos took was a couple of pounds of wool per sheep at each shearing, wool carefully woven by the women into Navajo blankets, a skill their ancestors had been taught by Pueblo men. About the same time, Navajo men became silver artisans in earnest. Originally learned by a Navajo under the tutelage of a New Mexican shortly before the Long Walk and then taught other Navajos, it was a craft for which Navajo artisans were to eventually become famous.

Both silver and blankets were subsequently traded for supplies at trading posts dotting the reservation, or better yet, for horses, the Navajos' ultimate symbol of wealth and esteem. By 1880 the Navajo sheep had increased to over 700,000 animals.

Yet, there was still hardship ahead. Drought often killed crops or grasshoppers stripped both cultivated plants and wild forage needed by livestock. Sometimes winters brought crippling snow accumulations, causing animals and humans alike to suffer.

Stock Reduction

Nonetheless, the Diné persevered, and by the turn of the century, their population had more than doubled, from roughly eight thousand when they left Bosque

Navajo Man

William M. Pennington, Durango Public Library

Redondo, to twenty thousand. Meanwhile, the sheep population increased to one million, goats to 250,000, horses to 100,500. But by the 1920s and 1930s that success brought new sadness to the Diné and greater hostility between Navajos and whites than anytime since the Long Walk.

The Navajo herds had simply grown until there were too many for the fragile desert of the Colorado Plateau. This was especially true since Navajos had been banished from the mountains and foothills in Colorado and along the eastern boundary of the traditional Diné Bikéyah in New Mexico. This largely ended the Navajos' centuries-old tradition of moving their animals into the high country in the summer, thus giving the desert a chance to heal itself.

Beyond the resulting overgrazing, the sharp, cutting hooves of tens of thousands of sheep and goats compacted the soil and killed vegetation. Meanwhile, the animals suffered too. Beginning in the 1880s, sheep were smaller and were producing less wool.

The effects of overgrazing can be seen to this day on many parts of the reservation. Very old Navajos, starring off into the distance in nostalgic reverie, remember a land much different from the sunburned expanses of the present. They remember a green land, a fertile steppe filled with flowers and butterflies, a land carpeted with relatively rich growths of plant life. Now, however, there are only elusive glimpses of that land of the past.

The busy highways cutting through the reservation have been fenced for the most part to prevent livestock from wandering into traffic. Sometimes at the crest of a hill, where it is possible to see miles of highway stretched out distorted and shimmering in the distance, a great, long band of green snakes across the land. This strip, protected by fences from grazing, is a disturbing reminder of the Colorado Plateau landscape of just a few generations ago.

Therefore, in the 1930s the U.S. government, vividly aware of the effects of erosion and the resulting Dust Bowl conditions of the Great Plains, decided that the Navajo herds must be reduced. They launched what was to become the hated federal Navajo Livestock Reduction Program that lasted from 1932 through 1942.

The reservation was divided into grazing districts and the number of animals that each district could realistically support was determined. The Navajos were then given quotas designating the number of animals they could own. Excess animals were sent to slaughter.

The Navajos were horrified at the loss of their animals. Financial compensation given them was of little value to a people who considered only animals to be a measure of wealth. Assurances that those which remained would be healthier and, therefore, more valuable were in vain. Further bitterness was sown with the tactless decision to sometimes allow white ranchers to graze their livestock on areas of the reservation where Navajo livestock numbers were being reduced. The Navajos were also enraged when 3,500 goats were shot and left to rot in the desert sun, a cheap alternative to sending them to distant slaughterhouses. Such waste and disregard for life was offensive to a people who believe that animals should only be killed to be eaten.

And sometimes stock reduction went to extremes. So many Navajo Churro sheep, an especially hardy breed known for its two-textured wool, were killed that the breed is still teetering on the brink of extinction.

And in spite of the heartbreak of stock reduction, most of the Navajo reservation continues to be overgrazed, contributing to depleted plant life and to the tragic spread of desertification. Some areas of the reservation, for example, are currently grazed by eight times as many animals as the land can realistically carry, causing destruction of protective plant life and extensive soil erosion.

Yet, in spite of bitterness caused by stock reduction, Navajo soldiers enlisted in the military and may have well helped turn the tied of World War II in the Pacific theater. The now-famous Navajo "Code Talkers" communicated strategic information in the Navajo language, confounding the Japanese, who thought they were dealing with a new form of code. Ironically, however, at the same time, Navajo children were being punished if they spoke Navajo at the government-operated boarding schools they were required to attend.

Today, with close to sixty percent unemployment on the reservation, poverty continues to be a major problem for a rapidly growing population of roughly 111,000 Navajos (1980 census).

In spite of construction on the reservation of some of the largest power plants in the world, which generate most of the electricity for Los Angeles, San Diego, Phoenix, Albuquerque, and Tucson; in spite of accompanying coal strip mines, which annually remove tons of energy resources from the reservation; in spite of a timber operation in the Chuska Mountains and construction of an enormous water project and associated agribusiness near Farmington, New Mexico, high unemployment continues. Meanwhile, environmental damage from strip mining, wells depleted by the removal of ground water for energy production, and air pollution from electric-power generation may be the *de facto* legacy of energy production for generations to come.

Yet, in spite of the problems of the late twentieth century, the Navajo tradition survives. A few hogans and ramadas still dot the desert. Some Navajos still live very much like their ancestors before them, often in regions so isolated that they are rarely visited by outsiders. Many still speak only Navajo and live nearly independent of a cash economy, surviving off the crops they grow, the animals they raise, and the small amount of money they make crafting silver or weaving blankets, which some Navajos increasingly sell not only to commercial outlets on and off the reservation, but astutely, directly to visitors to the reservation.

Sun and Earth

Equally surviving is the Diné's colorful religion.

The Navajos do not embrace the concept of life after death, believing instead that when an individual dies, while some corrupt ghostly remnants of his character may linger, he or she basically ceases to exist. In life, meanwhile, Navajos use a complicated series of songs,

Navajo Indian Irrigation Project

Kathleene Parker

chants, prayers, and herbal medicines to bring them into harmony with the natural forces of the universe or to bend those forces to their benefit.

Like the Pueblo people, the Navajos believe that everything has a spiritual essence. Moreover, that which nurtures and gives life to all things—Mother Earth—is a living, sentient being fostered in her work by the power of Father Sun or Father Sky. To the Navajos, everything in nature is male or female. Even the rain has its sex reflected in how it falls: heavy, pounding rain is a male rain; light, gentle rain is female rain.

Perhaps this reflects a culture where equality between the sexes is deeply ingrained. Clan lines, for example, run from one generation to the next through the woman's side of the family. A Navajo man will always proudly be part of his mother's clan, while Navajo women retain their names and family identity after marriage and control much of the family property, which is in turn inherited by their female descendants.

Meanwhile, in Navajo religion, the rainbow is the path of the Yei, "The Holy Ones," the offspring of Mother Earth and Father Sky. The Yei, incidentally, may be either good or evil and, like the Pueblo Kachinas, are impersonated during at least some important religious ceremonies.

The Navajo religion is a study in striving for harmony and a rapport between humankind and nature. All things in nature are believed to have powers, as reflected in certain traits of their being. The sun, moon, thunder, and water, for example, represent the power of motion; rocks, plants, and earth represent endurance and rejuvenation; and the coyote represents cunning and savvy, while other animals reflect various other personality traits. It is the Diné's task to evoke these powers to their benefit using elaborate chants.

Meanwhile, humankind exists on an equal plain with all other creatures and things. Similarly, there is no god of absolute power or authority in Navajo religion. While Father Sun may be considered to be a high god, without Changing Woman, who represents the changing seasons, and Mother Earth, he is powerless.

When a chant is needed, a visionary, a listener, a hand trembler, or a star gazer, one who has the ability to hear or to see revelations, is usually called upon to determine which chant is appropriate for a given set of circumstances. If someone is ill, different variations of religious ceremonies must be performed according to the type of illness. Those who become ill while around non-Navajos, for example, require the chanting of the Enemy Way. In each ceremony, the powers of the four sacred border mountains, as well as other sacred mountains and their deities, are invoked.

Each sacred chant, of which there are over fifty, has been passed down verbally in meticulous detail for countless generations. These ceremonies, some lasting several days, with their accompanying, "great mass of intricate ritual," as Western photographer and historian Laura Gilpin called it, must be performed in exact detail, for it is believed that sings were given to The People directly by the gods. Most chants are accompanied by specific sandpaintings, intricate geometric designs meticulously created with colored sands, pollens, seeds, vegetable matter, meal, and minerals according to a preestablished pattern. On these the gods are depicted, probably more than coincidentally looking like the masked Kachinas of the Pueblos, indication that the Navajo religion was very much influenced by the Pueblos.

Close to the conclusion of the sing, the person whom it is meant to benefit sits on the completed sandpainting and is believed to literally take on the powers of the supernatural forces depicted in it. He or she is cautioned not to touch others for fear of harming them. At the conclusion of the ceremony, he or she removes the supernatural powers by bathing in sacred yucca soap, and then acknowledges what the gods have done for him or her by arising early to "breathe in" the dawn. Finally, each sandpainting, although elaborate and beautiful, is disassembled in the reverse order of its creation to prevent any modification by witches in a way that might cause evil.

But beyond the ritual associated with a sing, it is an important social occasion, a time of fellowship and goodwill, sometimes attended by several hundred people.

The Navajos' religious ceremonies and chants, like their silver crafts and blankets, express their deep sense of aesthetics, as does the Nightway Chant, translated in the 1860s by Dr. Washington Matthews, a U.S. Army surgeon stationed at Fort Wingate, New Mexico. The beauty of the chant is lost only in the inadequacy of other languages to capture the minutiae and subtlety of the Navajo language.

> *"In Beauty (happily) I walk.*
> *With Beauty before me I walk.*
> *With Beauty behind me I walk.*
> *With Beauty below me I walk.*
> *With Beauty above me I walk.*
> *With Beauty all around me I walk.*
> *It is finished (again) in beauty.*
> *It is finished in beauty."*

Jicarilla Apache Braves
Colorado Historical Society

The Jicarilla Apaches

While the Apachu de Navajo dispersed across the Colorado Plateau, most other Apaches traveled into lands to the south to make their homes.

The Lipan Apaches settled in eastern New Mexico and West Texas, eventually moving into Mexico under pressure from the Comanches. The Mescalero Apaches, named after their love of eating the tender meat of the mescal cactus, lived in south, central New Mexico near the Sacramento Mountains. The Mimbreños lived along the Mimbres River in western New Mexico and were closely allied with the Chiricahua Apaches. The Chiricahuas lived in the Chiricahua Mountains of southeastern Arizona, in the Sierra Madres in the state of Chihuahua in Mexico, and in southwestern New Mexico.

The Western Apaches, meanwhile, consisted of the White Mountain Apaches, living along the southern rim of the Colorado Plateau in Arizona, and the Cibecue and San Carlos tribes, living slightly further south. The Western Apaches, were linguistically and culturally the most closely related to the Navajos, probably having separated from them only in the relatively recent past.

Undoubtedly the raiding tradition which brought tragedy to the Navajos also brought tragedy to the Apaches, particularly the Chiricahuas to the south of the Colorado Plateau.

The Mexican state of Chihuahua placed a bounty on the scalps of all Apache men, women, and children in 1837. This led to the slaughter not only of Apaches but of other Native Americans, even Mexicans, as bounty hunters harvested any scalp that might pass for that of an Apache.

When the U.S. government was victorious in its war with Mexico and assumed Mexican lands in the Southwest, the Apaches were delighted to be free of Mexican domination and felt special admiration for those who had driven the Mexicans out. That friendship ended quickly and bitterly, however, with the discovery of gold and silver on Apache lands.

As settlers and miners moved into the Arizona and New Mexico territories, they intruded upon Apache lands and demanded that the Apaches be removed. In 1871 a group of citizens from Tucson, Arizona, allied with Hispanics and nearby Papago Indians (today known as the Tohono ó otam people), historic enemies of the Apaches, attacked an Apache encampment while the Apache men were away on a hunting expedition. Upwards of 144 Apaches were murdered, all but eight of them women or children. President Grant demanded that the perpetrators be tried; however, after deliberating less than half-an-hour, a Tucson jury found the defendants not guilty of all charges.

Apaches were soon forced onto reservations, which were too small and too inhospitable for Apache self-sufficiency, thus forcing the Apaches to be dependant upon the government for supplies. When sporadic shipments did arrived, they were often inedible or inadequate.

The seeds of strife were sown.

Cochise and Geronino

The Chiricahuas, in particular, suffered. They were

placed on the San Carlos Indian Reservation in central Arizona, to the south of the Colorado Plateau, where temperatures frequently climbed above 120-degrees Fahrenheit. A military outpost there had earlier been abandoned because of outbreaks of malaria among the soldiers. The Apaches, especially the children, suffered and died. Some historians feel their placement at San Carlos was a deliberate attempt at extermination.

Ultimately, the Chiricahua leaders decided the Chiricahuas either had to flee the reservation or die. When they escaped and resumed their old raiding life in an attempt to survive, the outcry from white Americans was loud and frenzied. A Tucson newspaper, for example, called for attacks on the Apaches, "...until every valley and crest and crag and fastness shall send to high heaven the grateful incense of festering and rotting Chiricahuas."

Called by some the finest warriors North America ever saw, the Chiricahuas, led first by Cochise and then by Geronimo after Cochise's death in 1874, conducted a long and successful war against the U.S. and Mexican governments. Geronimo was not a hereditary chief, but in the democratic Apache tradition, had earned the right to lead his people based on his skills as a hunter and warrior. Also, like most Apache leaders, he was a spiritualist, who reportedly had psychic powers. Numbering only about twelve hundred people, the Chiricahuas hid out in the Chiricahua and Sierra Madre mountains and conducted a campaign of guerilla warfare, a last, desperate bid for freedom and dignity. Borne of their deep hatred of Anglos, they left a trail of blood across northern Mexico and the Arizona and New Mexico territories.

Geronimo's own stake in the conflict was not small; his mother, wife, and three small children had been murdered by Sonoran soldiers during a massacre of an Apache encampment near the town of Janos, Mexico, in 1850. Geronimo considered the attack ultimately cowardly since the soldiers had attacked only after ascertaining that no Apache warriors were in the area.

By the 1880s, thousands of Mexican troops and five thousand U.S. soldiers, almost a quarter of the U.S. Army, were charged with crushing the last handful of Chiricahuas. Ultimately, much of Geronimo's band was captured at its stronghold in the remote depths of the Sierra Madres, while Geronimo and his warriors were miles away. Tradition has it that spiritualist Geronimo had a vision of the capture of his people as it happened. He surrendered of his own accord some months later. In spite of his repeated pleas to be allowed to return home to die, he eventually died at Fort Sill, Oklahoma, after first enduring a prolonged exile in a Florida concentration camp.

Meanwhile, the Jicarilla Apaches of the Colorado Plateau suffered an only slightly less troubling fate.

The Apache de la Xicarilla

The *Apache de la Xicarilla*, "The People of the Baskets" or "Little Basket Makers," as the Spaniards called them, were named for the skill for which they are still known.

They ranged a homeland they believed was given them by *Black Hac c'i cin*, "The Creator," the omnipotent source of all supernatural power. That traditional homeland, although including much of southwestern Colorado's San Juan Mountains, rested for the most part beyond the boundaries of the Colorado Plateau. It also included the Sangre de Cristo mountains of southern Colorado and northern New Mexico and the Jemez and Sandia mountains of central New Mexico. From there, it extended eastward across the Colorado-New Mexico plains to Oklahoma.

Originally two distinct groups, the *Olleros*, "The Mountain People," and the *Llanero*, "The Plains People," the Jicarillas, who collectively called themselves the *Tinde*, "The People," were heavily influenced by the cultures of the Great Plains and the Pueblos. Like the people of the plains, they wore deerskin moccasins, lived in tepees made of animal skins sewn together and stretched over a frame of wooden poles, dressed in buckskin, and were hunter-gatherers. All were extraordinary horsemen, with girls, like boys, being taught not only to ride but to capture and to tame horses and to shoot bows and arrows.

The Jicarilla women did most of the gathering and were knowledgeable of an amazingly wide range of plants: which could be eaten, where they could be gathered, when they could be harvested, the medicinal qualities of each, and the non-food uses to which they could be put. The men, meanwhile, hunted, traveling far onto the plains to kill buffalo and antelope and into the mountains for deer, elk, and mountain sheep.

However, the western Jicarillas, the Olleros, "The Mountain People," had, like the Navajos, been heavily influenced by the Pueblo people, not only in the development of agriculture, but in some instances going so far as to abandon their tepees in favor of pueblo-type houses. Eventually, the Llanero of the plains also learned to practice horticulture to supplement the natural harvest of plants and animals.

The religion of Jicarillas, like that of the Navajos, was probably heavily influenced by the Pueblos. All three faiths embraced the idea of humankind emerging to the surface of this world from a world below, while the Jicarillas, like many of the Pueblos, participate even today in an annual sacred race. The Olleros, representing the sun and the animals, and the Llaneros, representing the moon and plants, meet in September for three days of religious preparation. Two kiva-like structures are built, one at each end of a race track, and sacred sandpaintings are made in concert with the recitation of sacred chants. If representatives of the Olleros win the race, it signifies that wild game will be abundant during the coming year, a Llaneros victory signifies that plants will be abundant. The Jicarillas, like the Pueblos and the Navajos, also observe puberty rites.

The arrival of the horse into the Jicarillas' lifeway, as in the instance of the Navajos and other Apaches, meant the addition of raiding to their culture, particularly against other plains-area peoples. Beyond that, the Jicarillas traded heavily with the Pueblos, who may have encouraged them and other Apaches to live nearby to help defend against the Spaniards.

The Colorado Plateau

When Jicarilla lands were part of the Mexican frontier, isolation and a comparative lack of resources attracted little attention to them. However, when the homeland became part of the U.S., a wholesale influx of settlers began.

Thus, the Jicarillas found themselves rapidly being pushed from their traditional lands and deprived of their livelihood. As they tried to become more dependant upon agriculture, drought repeatedly killed their crops. Facing the very real possibility of starvation, they stepped up raids for cattle. But as more settlers arrived and hostilities increased, the Jicarillas finally became totally dependant upon the government for food rations.

Acting Governor William S. Messervy of the Territory of New Mexico stated in 1854 that "...the best interests of this territory and the highest dictates of humanity demanded their (the Jicarillas') extinction."

By that time, the Jicarillas were begging that a reservation be set aside for them, a proposal to which many New Mexicans were opposed, in part because they profited economically from the presence of the military and the large number of troops required to keep peace in the region. Each time a new area of land for a reservation was targeted by the government, at least some New Mexicans launched either real or fictitious claims to the land. In another instance, a proposal for a reservation in the San Juan Mountains was terminated when gold was discovered there.

The Jicarillas were ultimately ordered to at least temporarily join the Mescalero Apaches on a reservation in southern New Mexico. After a comparatively short time there, however, the Jicarillas, homesick for northern New Mexico and frustrated by their inability to grow crops with water which was too alkaline, quietly went home and refused to return to the reservation even when ordered to do so.

Finally, at the urging of the Ute chief, Ouray, the half-brother of a Jicarilla leader, a Jicarilla delegation traveled to Washington, D.C., to directly ask President Grover Cleveland to establish a reservation for them, a request supported by a military eager to have squabbles between whites and the Jicarillas resolved. The reservation was established by executive order in 1887.

Ironically, it was only through the formation of this reservation that the Jicarilla Apaches moved to the extreme eastern edge of the Colorado Plateau, on lands adjoining the Navajo reservation. The Jicarilla reservation was established in two main sections, the original northern section in 1887 and a later southern section in 1908. These lands extend from the Colorado-New Mexico border, more-or-less along the Continental Divide of the southern San Juan Mountains, south to near Cuba, New Mexico, near but not including most of the Jicarillas' original homeland.

The Suffering Continues

Even with the establishment of their dreamed-of reservation, however, the Jicarillas suffering was far from over.

Anglo settlers intruded onto the reservation, taking

the best lands and leaving the Jicarillas those lacking water or at elevations too high for agriculture. And while timber from the reservation was being sold by the government and the profits deposited in the U.S. treasury in non-interest-bearing accounts, the Jicarillas starved. Meanwhile, the entire southern half of the reservation was leased by the U.S. government to whites for livestock grazing.

The malnourished, poverty-stricken people were ravaged by disease. Tuberculosis, measles, trachoma, and influenza took their toll. From 824 people in 1891, the Jicarilla population plummeted to 588 by 1920. Health problems were ironically compounded by the Jicarillas' years-long fight for educational facilities for their children. When schools were finally built, disease spread from the schools outward into the community, often because of mismanagement. One public health official discovered, for example, that drinking water at one school was muddy and contained dead mice.

Not until the 1930s and the passage of the Indian Reorganization Act did the Jicarillas' lot improve. That act worked to remove those who had intruded onto reservation lands and to consolidate Native American holdings. It also moved the U.S. government away from a paternalistic attitude, and for the first time recognized the full rights of citizenship for Native Americans under the U.S. Constitution. As Native Americans, including the Jicarillas, began to slowly have control over their own resources and their own destinies, their lot improved, although years of poverty have left a deep, perhaps indelible, mark on them.

The Jicarillas, numbering roughly two thousand people as of the 1980 census, have carved an economy from livestock and timber production and energy-resource royalties, as well as from financial restitution made to them by the U.S. government under the Indian Claims Act of 1946 for lands unlawfully taken during the nineteenth century.

Havasupai Woman With Child in Burden Basket

U.S. Department of the Interior, Grand Canyon National Park, Identification Number 5117

The Pai

The Grand Canyon. It is beyond a doubt the most stupendous canyon on Earth, a mile deep, phenomenally beautiful, unbelievably rugged, so immense as to almost defy comprehension.

Amazingly, humankind has lived in and around that craggy chasm for thousands of years.

People of the Paleo-Indian culture hunted in the area around eleven thousand years ago, while people of the Desert Archaic culture were probably in the area 7,500 years ago. "Split-twig" figurines, representing deer, antelope, and bighorn sheep, have been found stashed in caves in the canyon, probably left there by wandering hunters ten thousand to twelve thousand years ago.

About 600 A.D. the Cohonina people began to settle on the Cohonina Plateau along the South Rim of the canyon, while the Basketmaker Anasazi settled mostly on the North Rim. The Cohonina culture was somewhat similar to that of the Basketmaker, although much simpler. The Cohonina lived in unadorned stone or wood houses, but for only part of the year, and they had no kivas or other religious structures. But by about 900 A.D., pressures from the thriving Anasazi culture forced the Cohonina to move to the western end of the Cohonina Plateau, where their culture died out, perhaps absorbed by surrounding peoples, perhaps forced from the region entirely, or perhaps compelled to move into the depths of the canyon where they became the ancestors of Havasupai people.

And now, the Pai are the people of the canyon.

Presently, there are three major groups of Pai people, the Havasupai, living at the bottom of the Grand Canyon;

the Hualapai (also spelled Walapai), living immediately south of the western end of the Grand Canyon; and the historic enemies of both peoples, the Yavapai, living beyond the boundaries of the Colorado Plateau to the south of the Bill Williams River in west, central Arizona. All have probably lived in the region for thousands of years. The Havasupai and Hualapai, each consisting of several bands, thought of themselves as being of the same tribe—"The Only True People on Earth"—until the 1860s. But then they were forced onto two different reservations by the U.S. government, which classified them separately and at least legally split the tribe. All of the Pai people speak the Yuman language, indigenous to the Colorado River region of southwestern Arizona, extreme southern California, and northwestern Mexico.

The Desert Culture

Before the 1860s, the Colorado Plateau Pai people consisted of a dozen or so bands living south of and in the Grand Canyon, pursuing a lifeway that was one of the strongest surviving examples of the Desert culture. They practiced a modified seasonal round, moving to the river bottoms and protected canyons to plant crops during the summer and then scattering across the countryside in winter to hunt and gather. Each band had a specific area to which it laid claim, and each was known by a name descriptive of the place where it spent most of the seasonal round.

Thus, the Havasupai were known as "The People of the Blue-Green Water," a name descriptive of the color of the water of Havasu Creek, as it flows toward the Colorado River just below that river's confluence with the Little Colorado. There, in the depths of the Grand Canyon, in a place that American explorer Frank H. Cushing in 1881 called, "a veritable land of summer," the Havasupai raised corn, beans, squash, peaches, apricots, cotton, tobacco, and sunflowers irrigated with the waters of Havasu Creek. Following the annual harvest celebration in late summer or early fall, a large, tremendously important religious and social occasion attended by people from miles around, the Havasupai climbed to the pine-, juniper-, and pinyon-carpeted canyon rim. There the women gathered seeds, nuts, berries, roots, and plants, while the men hunted deer, antelope, desert bighorn sheep, and rabbits.

Part of the ultimate product of such hunts, buckskin, along with salt from the Grand Canyon, and ochre, a dye derived from iron ore found in the canyon, were frequently traded to the nearby Hopis for a wide range of goods the Hopis had acquired from throughout the Southwest.

Meanwhile, some bands of the Hualapai or "Pine Springs People," practiced agriculture in the western extremes of the Grand Canyon, while still others cultivated crops along the Colorado River below the canyon. These lands were part of the Pai's traditional realm, a land which they believed had been set aside for them by divine intercession. The Pai homeland stretched from the eastern shore of the Colorado River, as it turns southward toward Mexico after leaving the Grand Canyon, eastward along the Bill Williams River, and then across the Cohonina Plateau to the distant San Francisco Peaks. Hindered by the region's dry climate, some bands farmed only sporadically and were largely dependant upon hunting and gathering, although they sometimes also traded sea shells, acquired from the peoples of coastal areas of California and western Mexico, with the Hopis for needed goods.

During the more settled months of their semi-sedentary existence, the Pai lived in loosely organized villages near their gardens. Their houses were dome-shaped huts made of poles, bark, and branches; small square-shaped dwellings made of poles and brush; or small, square- or rectangular-shaped stone structures.

Each band was led by a headman, who had little authority and who, therefore, had to lead by persuasion or by simply earning the respect of his followers. In the Pai's very unstructured day-to-day existence, little tribal authority or influence was wanted or permitted. While the eligibility to be a headman was inherited, the actual right to lead was granted based on ability, or sometimes, the wishes of a previous headman who had recommended a successor.

Like many other people of the Colorado Plateau, the Havasupai and Hualapai adopted elements of the Pueblo religion, specifically masked dancing, rain dances, and prayer sticks for prayers to the sun, Earth, water, and rocks. They believed in life after death and in ghosts, and they believed in the ability of spiritual leaders—shamans—to cure diseases and injuries and to influence the weather. The historical Pai cremated the dead and all of the possessions of the dead. They also annually burned food, clothing, and other possessions in a ceremony honoring the dead.

Gold and Tragedy

The Pai's first contact with white men occurred perhaps as early as 1598, but more probably between 1662 and 1670, while Spanish missionaries lived at Oraibi on the Hopi mesas. Yet, contact with outsiders in the rugged, isolated lands of northern Arizona was minimal until gold was discovered on Pai lands in the Hualapai and Cerbat mountains in 1865. That was the beginning of the end for an age-old way of life.

Miners soon swarmed across Pai lands, blocking access to critical hunting, gathering, and planting areas. The miners were followed by cattlemen, who often denied the Pai access to the sparse scattering of springs and water holes or whose animals fouled water supplies or destroyed crops. Astutely, some of the Pai began to exchange woven goods, acquired from the Pueblos, with the Mohave people of southern Arizona for horses and weapons. Finally, after months of increasing tension, Hualapai chief Wauba Yuma was killed by prospectors and the Hualapai Wars of the 1860s were underway.

By the late 1860s, however, the Hualapai and their southern-Arizona kin, the Yavapai, had been defeated by the U.S. Army. The Hualapai faced a tragic one-year internment at La Paz on the lower Colorado River, where many of them, accustomed to the cooler temperatures on the high plateau near the Grand Canyon, died from the stifling heat. Although allowed to leave La Paz, not until 1883 was a reservation formally established for them on the Hualapai Plateau near Peach Springs, Arizona, on lands only a fraction of the size of their original domain.

The Havasupai, meanwhile, avoided confronting the white man, instead withdrawing into the isolation of the Grand Canyon. There, in the 1880s, out of their original enormous historic homeland, they were granted 518 acres as a reservation. Meanwhile, the use of both the Hualapai's and Havasupai's historic gathering lands was radically curtailed, bringing their seasonal round to an abrupt end and subjecting them to complete destitution and dependance upon government-supplied rations. Poverty and disease very nearly decimated both peoples. In 1881, for example, there were an estimated 214 Havasupai, but by 1890 that had dropped to 166.

Today, the Hualapai economy is based on livestock, timber harvesting, and limited farming, and the number who can live on the reservation is severely restricted by a lack of economic opportunities. Thus, of a tribe numbering roughly nine hundred people (1980 census), only about five hundred now live on ancestral lands.

The Havasupai, now numbering about five hundred people with about three hundred of those living on the reservation, continue to farm, but due to the restricted size of their farmlands must also travel to the canyon rim to do mostly unskilled work in the forestry, cattle, and tourist industries or to provide pack trains into the canyon. Recently, the Havasupai have encouraged limited tourism at tribal-owned facilities in the Grand Canyon.

Paiute Women

1871-1872 Powell Expedition, Colorado Historical Society

The Southern Paiutes

In the not so distant past, the Southern Paiutes traveled the western-most extremes of the Colorado Plateau, like the Pai people, living a nearly intact form of the Desert culture. In lands in and near the spectacularly beautiful Zion and Bryce canyon regions of southwestern Utah and deep into the Arizona Strip, that portion of Arizona north of the Grand Canyon, they lived the seasonal round.

Their simple hunting-gathering existence was aptly suited to the beautiful but extremely harsh lands upon which they lived. They traveled in small, mobile family groups, so that too many people would not demand too much of any one place on the land for too long. They hunted with bows made of chokecherry limbs. The bows were wrapped in sinew affixed with glue derived by boiling the hooves of recently killed animals. Arrow tips, meanwhile, were dipped into poison to expedite the kill.

They had shamans (medicine men), who were believed to have healing powers and who it was thought influenced the weather. Each shaman gained his supernatural powers in a dream or vision, and each specialized in treating a particular kind of illness. The Paiutes, more than attributing special powers to shamans directly, believed that they were an instrument through which *Ahppu*, "The Creator," worked.

The Paiutes, a term of unknown origins which may mean, "True Utes," lived mostly in temporary brush shelters erected along their routes of travel, although often in summer no shelters were used at all. They made simple brown to reddish-brown pottery, with cone-shaped bottoms, and wove burden baskets, hats, and coiled baskets out of native plants. Their simple, migratory lifestyle left little need for structured religious or social organization, and leadership, what little was needed, was determined not by heredity but by an individual's ability to convince others that he was worthy of being a leader.

And the Paiutes affixed often colorful and descriptive names to the features of the Colorado Plateau landscape. They, for example, named the Zion Canyon cul-de-sac, *Ioogoon*, "Arrow Quiver," or "Leave the Way You Entered," and Bryce Canyon with its thousands of strangely shaped "hoodoo" rock formations, *Unka-timpe-wa-wince-pock-ich*, "Red Rocks Standing Like People in a Bowl-Shaped Canyon."

They ate prairie dogs, ground squirrels, rabbits, fish (a dietary taboo of the Apaches or Navajos), deer, antelope, elk, pinon nuts, grass seeds, and some forms of insects and insect larvae, a practice that was to later earn them the contemptuous nickname, "Digger Indians," from American settlers and prospectors. Nonetheless, the Paiute had learned to survive, even to thrive, on a land where several Spanish exploration parties barely avoided starvation.

The Southern Paiutes were part of the much larger Paiute tribe, who spoke a Shoshonean dialect of the Uto-Aztecan language and who in prehistory lived throughout the Great Basin region of southern California, southeastern Oregon, southwestern Idaho, northwestern Utah, and throughout Nevada. They were linguistically closely related to other Shoshonean-speaking people, including the Utes of Utah and Colorado; the Comanches of the Great Plains; the Hopis of northern Arizona; the Papagos of south, central Arizona; the Pimas of southern Arizona and northern Mexico; the Shoshones of California, Nevada, and Idaho; and the Tarahumaras and Nahuatls of Mexico. The Uto-Aztecan language was, in other words, spoken from Idaho to the Isthmus of Tehuantepec and from the Great Plains to the Pacific.

The Southern Paiutes may have been descendants of the mysterious Fremont people, who lived upon the Colorado Plateau fifteen hundred years ago or more, or they may have moved into the northern areas of the American Southwest from the Great Basin around 1,000 A.D. The Southern Paiutes' ancestors apparently lived peacefully alongside the Anasazi until competition for limited resources may have caused discord and may have at least contributed to the Anasazi exodus.

Nonetheless, the two peoples apparently lived peacefully for many generations. In fact, the Anasazi may have taught the Paiutes their first agricultural skills, triggering a change in Paiute lifestyle from totally hunting-gathering to semi-sedentary. Under Anasazi influence, the Paiutes became agricultural to the extent that they learned to plant crops in the spring and returned to harvest them in the fall.

The Strangers Arrive

The Paiutes' first recorded glimpse of whites occurred near what is now Cedar City, Utah, on October 10th, 1776, when the Escalante-Domínguez expedition, trying unsuccessfully to find an overland route from Santa Fe to the California coast, came across a family of Paiutes. Of the Paiute women's sparse traditional attire, the scandalized Escalante, a priest, wrote, "(It) hardly covered that what can not be looked upon without peril."

In 1869 explorer John Wesley Powell conducted the first expedition down the Green and Colorado rivers. Unaware that they were nearly through the Grand Canyon, three of Powell's men, despairing of ever completing the journey through the canyon on the river, left the expedition and climbed to the canyon rim. There they encountered a party of Southern Paiutes, who were searching for a group of miners who had raped and murdered a Paiute woman. Not believing that it was possible to travel through the formidable canyon by boat and not believing it likely that there could be two groups of Americans in the isolated region at the same time, the Paiutes killed Powell's men, believing them to be the murderers. Later, they apologized to Powell for their grievous error.

Historically Paiute lands had been mostly ignored by Spain and Mexico and with the exception of some Paiutes captured and sold as slaves, the Paiutes had remained largely free of harassment by Spaniards and Mexicans. The entry of American settlers, however, brought extreme hardship, in part because of the Americans' total ignorance of how to live upon the harsh, fragile lands of the Colorado Plateau.

As Mormon settlers poured into Utah and as settlers and miners traveled through the region on the way to California, their livestock and horses competed with wild game for sparse grazing. Further, the settlers killed many game animals, radically reducing game populations and upsetting the delicate balance which had allowed the Paiutes to survive on marginal lands. Meanwhile, as Mormon ranchers fanned across Utah and northern Arizona, they demanded the greenest valleys with the most—sometimes the only—dependable supplies of water, thus shutting the Southern Paiutes out from areas where they had grown crops for generations.

Fortunately, however, much of the violence Native Americans had faced elsewhere from settlers was tempered by Mormon leader Brigham Young's admonition to his people, "It is better to feed them (the Paiutes) than to fight them." This not only prevented bloodshed, but gave the Paiutes a place to turn for help as they began to lose their self-sufficiency and face hunger. Also, the Mormons were eager to teach the Paiutes new agricultural techniques. The Paiutes, seeing the Mormons' enormous harvests, in some instances actually sought the opportunity to live near them in order to learn. Others, however, fled to live among the Northern Paiutes in order to distance themselves from Mormon proselytizing.

The settlers sometimes also unwittingly brought catastrophe to the Paiutes. In one instance near Kanab, Utah, for example, after contact with white settlers, one hundred Southern Paiutes died of measles within a few days, a devastating toll for a people who probably numbered only a thousand or so to begin with.

By 1855 tensions between settlers and the Paiutes became especially critical. A massive drought killed most of the crop of grass seed, a staple of the Paiute diet. The grass seed had become increasingly critical with the loss of traditional hunting and farming lands. In an attempt to protect native grasses and as an alternative food source, the Paiutes killed ever more of the settlers' livestock, but then they learned from the Plains Indians that more settlers were headed west "like locusts" and that fighting the onslaught was futile.

In 1873 John Wesley Powell wrote of the Southern Paiutes, "They fully understand that the settlement of the country by white men is inevitable...Their hunting-grounds have been spoiled, their favorite valleys are occupied by white men, and they are compelled to scatter in small bands in order to obtain sustenance."

The Dance of Hope

It was during these times that the Ghost Dance came to the Southern Paiutes and many other Native American tribes of the West and Great Plains. In 1869 a Northern Paiute mystic by the name of Wodziwob claimed to have had a vision in which the old white-dominated world ended. Afterward, dead Native Americans—the only true people—along with the buffalo, returned to a world that was again free and fertile and nurturing. For this vision to come to be, Wodziwob instructed his followers to sing certain songs, perform ritual dances, and wear symbolic costumes. The movement spread like wildfire among indigenous people living across the entire western half of the United States.

When the rituals did not bring about the healing of the

Paiute Woman

U.S. Department of the Interior, Grand Canyon National Park, Identification Number 5993

land by the time foretold, the movement lost momentum. However, with the continuing Native American tragedies in the 1880s, the Ghost Dance experienced a resurgence under another Northern Paiute, Wovoka. Some Native Americans, particularly the Sioux, even believed that if they wore "ghost shirts," supposedly impervious to bullets, they would be protected from injury. Apprehension about the movement caused the U.S. government to direct the military to bring a halt to Ghost Dances. This eventually led to tragedy when three hundred Sioux, including women and children, were massacred by the U.S. Army at Wounded Knee, South Dakota, as they gathered for a Ghost Dance.

Thus, the last hope of resuming the old way of life died for the Southern Paiutes and other Native Americans.

Soon, in a tragic repetition of events, the Southern Paiutes were relegated to reservations, where they became largely dependant upon government rations. In the poverty and filth in which they were forced to live, illness took a major toll. In the 1920s, for example, the Southern Paiutes' Northern Paiute kin on the Pyramid Lake reservation in Nevada suffered from active tuberculosis at a rate of 327 per one thousand, the highest of any Native Americans and a rate many times higher than among Anglos at the same time.

Ironically, in the 1950s, the U.S. government in a baffling decision which seems to defy logic, declared the Shivwits Paiute incapable of handling the affairs of a reservation and ordered a Utah bank to sell off all reservation lands. However, the property was so poor and so lacking in water that no buyer was ever found. The Shivwits Paiute people, meanwhile, uneducated, illiterate, and cut off from all government benefits, entered abject, total poverty, eking out a pathetic existence living on the fringes of communities in southern Utah and northern Arizona. Later, the Shivwits reservation was reinstated.

Like many Native Americans, the Southern Paiutes benefited from monies gained from the U.S. government under the Indian Claims Act of 1946. They were finally compensated in the 1970s for lands taken from them during the nineteenth century, revenues which allowed the tribe to establish a small but dependable source of income for its people and create some economic opportunities on the reservations.

The Southern Paiutes, as of 1980 numbering roughly fifteen hundred people, are engaged in cattle ranching, usually with tribal-owned herds, farming, and some tourism. They derive additional income by subletting tourist-oriented businesses on their reservations. There has also been some revival of Paiute crafts, particularly basketmaking, but many Paiutes are still dependant upon wage work off the reservations.

Chief Ouray
Colorado Historical Society

The Utes

The Ute people once wandered an enormous and varied domain, encompassing mountains, plains, and desert, as they lived the seasonal round. Like all hunter-gatherers, they needed a huge area of land to support their way of life.

The Utes have long lived upon the Colorado Plateau and neighboring regions, like the Paiutes, to whom they are closely related, speaking a Shoshonean dialect of the Uto-Aztecan language and living, at least prior to the arrival of the Spaniards, a fairly pure form of the Desert culture.

They believed in a supreme being, *Manitou,* "The Great Spirit," whose powers were associated with the sun. A bisexual male-female deity, Manitou created all life and all things and was, interestingly enough, also worshipped by the indigenous people of the Great Lakes region of the north, central United States. The Utes also believed in lesser gods, whose powers were subordinate to Manitou, and in life after death, when their spirits would travel to live with the sun in a place where there was no sickness, pain, or suffering—only happiness. The animals too, the Utes believed, went to the same paradise.

Every morning when the Utes arose to begin the day, they faced the rising sun, took its warmth into their hands and "poured" the warmth over their bodies in ritual greeting. Religion for the Utes was an extremely personal experience involving oneness with the natural world and requiring no religious hierarchy to achieve that communion.

Perhaps the descendants of the early Fremont people or perhaps descendants of a people who split off from the main body of the early Basketmaker Anasazi, the Utes may have been part of the long-ago Desert Archaic culture and may have lived in the Colorado Plateau region for ten thousand years or more. Or they may have been descendants of a nomadic people who filtered into the Southwest from the north while the Anasazi lived in the Four Corners area. They eventually occupied virtually all mountain regions of Colorado and are in fact the longest continuous residents of that state. They also inhabited most of Utah, which is named after them, as well as a small area of extreme southern Wyoming and part of extreme northern New Mexico.

In times past, as spring came, the Utes split into small family groups, often consisting of only a husband and wife, their children, and perhaps at least one set of the children's grandparents, and followed deer and elk as the animals began to move from the lower foothills up into the high mountains for the summer. There the Utes remained, living mostly off animals hunted with bows and arrows or lances and off fishing, until wild plants began to reach their mid- to late-summer maturity. A natural harvest of berries, nuts, seeds, and plants was then gathered. As the first touches of gold and orange began to tinge the aspen trees in the autumn, the deer and elk—and the Utes—turned to move back into the sheltered lower valleys of the foothills or to the edge of the desert, with the Utes, at least in a few instances, stopping along the way to harvest crops they had planted in the spring.

There in the low country, the many small individual

families which had earlier dispersed across the countryside came together again to spend the winter with other families of their band, seven of which, at least in historical times, formed the Ute tribe. Each loosely structured band concentrated its movements within specific locales.

The Ute bands, together perhaps totaling upwards of ten thousand people, consisted of the Mouache band, living in southern Colorado and northern New Mexico along the Sangre de Cristo Mountains; the Capote band, living in the San Luis Valley in Colorado and along the Chama and Rio Grande rivers of extreme northern New Mexico; the Weminuche, living in and near the southern San Juan Mountains of southwestern Colorado and northwestern New Mexico; the Tabeguache or Uncompahgre, living in or near the northern San Juans; the Parianuc or Grand River Utes, living along the Colorado River in western Colorado and eastern Utah; the Yampa band, along the Yampa River in northwestern Colorado; and the Uintah band, in the Uintah Basin in east, central Utah and the Wasatch and Uinta mountains of northeastern Utah.

While the Utes collectively called themselves, the *Nuche,* "The People," the Shoshoni and Comanche people called them, *Yuuttaa* or *Yutah,* a term which has never been precisely translated. In the early 17th century, Spanish Governor Luis de Rosas of Santa Fe corrupted the Shoshoni and Comanche name and reported the capture of eighty "Uticahs," a term which eventually evolved to simply, "Uintas," "Utahs," or "Utes."

When the members of the bands rendezvoused in winter, it was a time of great socializing after the relative solitude and isolation of the summer. Extended families reunited, friendships were renewed, goods were traded, social events were held.

During the summer, the Utes required little or no shelter, like other people of the Great Basin, using only "wickiups," consisting of a frame of wooden poles covered with brush and reeds. However, in winter they lived in tepees, an adaptation from the Plains Indians.

With the return of spring, the Bear Dance, the most ancient Ute dance, was held at that time of year when bears emerge from their dens after the winter hibernation. Depicted in ancient petroglyphs found in the Uinta Mountains of Utah and even in Fremont rock art, the Bear Dance was a social occasion of tremendous importance. For three days and three nights, the dancers danced, face-to-face, men in a line to the north, women in a line to the south, within the boundary of a large circle. Finally, at noon on the third day, the women "pushed" the men from the circle to the north by dancing toward them. The dance then ended with a feast. It was also during the Bear Dance, immediately prior to the band again dispersing into the high country, that most Ute marriages occurred.

Horses, Freedom, Opportunity

But a radical change came to this age-old lifeway when the Utes acquired horses from the Spaniards.

The Utes had previously transported their possessions on travois, pulled by women or dogs to the

Ute Tepees, Durango, Colorado

Colorado Historical Society

next place of encampment. Such moves were a slow, arduous process. Horses, however, brought the Utes new mobility.

For the first time, they found it realistic to frequently journey significant distances from the mountains to hunt the much-valued buffalo of the Great Plains, and for the first time, horses quickly and expeditiously carried burdens from one campsite to the next. It was also possible to leave women and children in much more distant and protected locales when engaging enemies in battle. But most important, it was no longer necessary for the Utes to scatter over vast areas of land in small family units to hunt and to gather. For the first time, they could remain congregated year around in large numbers. Because the people could remain together and develop greater cohesion and social structure, their leaders came to have more influence.   And like most of the Native Americans of the region, the Utes became raiders in earnest, attacking other tribes, especially Plains Indians and Navajos, as well as isolated ranches and small settlements in the Colorado and Utah mountains. From these the Utes took horses to ride, herd animals to eat, and captives to sell as slaves.

Very quickly, horses became of paramount importance to the Utes. And with the acquisition of horses and the resulting greater mobility, the Ute culture, previously influenced mostly by the Desert culture, began to be much more profoundly influenced by the Plains culture, and to a lesser degree, by the cultures of the Pueblo and Navajo people.

But then came the 1850s and the beginning of the end of the Ute lifeway.

Time of Sorrows

Gold was discovered at Cripple Creek, Colorado, near present-day Colorado Springs in the 1850s, sparking the Pike's Peak gold rush. Compounded by the extreme dislocations caused by the U.S. Civil War, hordes of miners and settlers swarmed into the Colorado Territory, then to demand the removal of Colorado Plains Indians and of the Utes.

At the beginning of the influx, the Ute chief Ouray (pronounced "YOU-ray" and meaning "Arrow") had predicted, "We shall fall as the leaves from the trees when winter comes, and the lands we have roamed for countless generations will be given to the miner and the plowshare...and we shall be buried out of sight."

Somehow Ouray, of the Uncompahgre band, was able to see the futility of the Ute's situation in the mid-nineteenth century and the implications of the sheer numbers of people about to descend upon his land. The series of treaties made with the Utes and broken in rapid succession was perhaps one of the most profound examples of the lack of good faith extended by the U.S. government toward the Native Americans.

As the Colorado Territory was settled, pressure grew for the removal of the Utes from twenty million acres of Colorado. Colorado Governor Frederick Pitkin said, "My idea is that unless removed by the government, they must be exterminated...." Simultaneously, covert warfare was waged upon the Native Americans, as whites set out to slaughter the buffalo in the hopes that the animals' extinction would also mean the end of the Indians who depended upon them.

Meanwhile, many Plains Indians either lived or hunted in eastern Colorado: Cheyenne, Arapahoe, Kiowas, Kiowa Apaches (an Apache group who had long ago settled with Kiowas living in the Black Hills of South Dakota), Shoshones, Pawnees, and Sioux. (The Comanches had already moved from the region by about 1800.) Some Plains Indians attacked white settlements in an attempt to drive out the strangers who were inundating their lands. Nonetheless, the Utes remained mostly at peace, in no small part due to the vision and determination of their half-Jicarilla Apache, half-Ute chief, Ouray, who recognized the futility of resisting white settlement. U.S. President Rutherford Hayes once said of him, "Ouray is the most intellectual man I have ever conversed with."

Meanwhile, under the Treaty of 1868, the Utes were forced to move well back from the population centers that had sprung up along Colorado's Front Range. This cost them the valuable parkland regions of central and northern Colorado, as well as the San Luis Valley in south, central Colorado. However, the remaining western portion of the state, approximately sixteen million acres, was to be theirs, according to the treaty, "for as long as the rivers run and the grasses grow," primarily because whites considered those lands to be worthless.

However, only a few months later, gold was discovered in the San Juan Mountains, and the U.S. government, helpless to halt the mad influx of gold-obsessed prospectors, insisted that the Utes sign a new treaty ceding the entire San Juan Mountains. The Utes were probably lied to when they signed the agreement, the Brunot Treaty of 1873, most likely believing that they were signing away only those lands with mines actually located upon them.

In the late 1870s, public opinion was turned even further against the Utes, when Indian agent Nathan Meeker and eight other men were killed in a Ute uprising at Meeker, Colorado. Young Utes were angered that promised government supplies had not been delivered. Meeker then inflamed the situation when he ordered a track for Ute horse racing plowed under. As the young Utes became increasingly angry, Meeker overreacted and sent for troops. Tensions escalated until the Utes attacked the agency, killing the men and taking three women and two children hostage for twenty-three days. Meanwhile, the troops summoned to the scene by Meeker were also attacked and thirteen soldiers killed.

The Meeker uprising increased the outcry for the Utes' removal from Colorado, fear and hatred fanned in no small part by yellow journalism. Newspapers found that they could profit from sensationalism and even blatant distortion of Native American actions. In print, Native Americans were invariably portrayed as villains, whites as virtuous heros or put-upon victims.

Meanwhile, Ouray had tried to work constructively with white authorities. He wanted his people to at least retain hunting rights to large areas of Utah and Colorado, even if they were denied access to more settled locales and were no longer permitted to live in other areas. With

Ute Woman and Children, Denver, Colorado; October 17, 1895

Durango Public Library

the Meeker incident, he correctly realized that his people would be forced onto reservations and denied their old hunting grounds—and with them their freedom and self-sufficiency.

Coincidentally, the Meeker Massacre has lived in strange infamy in Colorado compared with the so-called Sand Creek "incident." Although camped south of Pueblo, Colorado, in a full state of surrender, four hundred to five hundred mostly unarmed Cheyenne and Arapaho people (no one ever knew for sure how many) were attacked by the Colorado Volunteers, the volunteer army of the Colorado Territory, during the early morning hours of November 29th, 1864. Few of the Cheyenne or Arapaho survived, and in the belief that "nits make lice," even small children and infants were killed, their scalps taken to be hung on soldiers' belts as souvenirs.

When the full details of the attack finally emerged, there was a public outcry, particularly in the eastern U.S., about the wholesale murder of the mostly unarmed people; however, that indignation resulted in few reforms of Indian policy nor did it significantly change attitudes which demanded the Native Americans' removal from their native lands. Settlers in the West, in particular, continued to be determined to be entirely rid of the indigenous people.

The Reservations

Finally in the 1880s with many Coloradans galled that the Utes still occupied so much valuable land, yet another treaty was negotiated. It further reduced the Ute domain, relegating Colorado and northern New Mexico Utes to a 15-mile-wide, 140-mile-long parcel of land south of the San Juan Mountains, the so-called Ute Strip. The Ute Strip ran parallel to the Colorado-New Mexico border, in one area reaching slightly into northern New Mexico.

Meanwhile, most Utah Utes had been forced onto the Uintah reservation at Fort Duchesne east of Salt Lake City in the early 1860s. Following the Meeker Massacre, the Yampa, Uncompahgre, and Grand River bands, Colorado's so-called Northern Utes, were also removed to the Uintah reservation. However, because of overcrowding and resulting friction between the Utes, a separate section of the Uintah reservation, the Ouray extension, east of the Green River in the area of Desolation Canyon, was created for Colorado's Northern Utes. That brought the northern Utah reservation to a total of 1.3 million acres. Life on the Utah reservation, a wind-blown, semi-desert region, represented a difficult transition for the Northern Utes, particularly the Uncompahgre band, who were use to the lush, green mountains and foothills of western Colorado.

From an enormous area spanning much of two states, the Utes were thus relegated to two comparatively small reservations. The old lifeway was dead. There were no more valleys in which to hunt, no more fertile mountainsides upon which to harvest plants in the ways of old. Once one of the most self-sufficient people in the world, the Utes were relegated to handouts from the U.S. government.

But there was more to come. In 1885 the Hunter Act

passed Congress. It awarded private land ownership to individuals within the tribe for purposes of farming, usually 160 acres for a Ute family, lesser plots for individual Utes. However, to appease whites who wanted even the reservations abolished and the land given over to whites, remaining lands were considered surplus and were opened to homesteading. Soon, even the Ute reservations were broken up and checkerboarded with the 160-acre plots of homesteaders.

Chief Ignacio of southwestern Colorado's Weminuche band, however, feared that such a policy would result in the total destruction of the Weminuches' historically communal lifestyle. He and his people adamantly refused to participate in the allotment program and in becoming the farmers that it implied. Instead, they were allowed to move to 553,000 acres at the extreme western end of the Ute Strip. These holdings, including 107,000 acres of Ute Strip lands in New Mexico, were protected for the Weminuche by a ban on homesteading.

Thus, the Ute Strip was split in half and divided into two separate reservations, the Southern Ute reservation, headquartered out of Ignacio, Colorado, and consisting mostly of the Moache and Capote bands; and the western reservation, the Ute Mountain Ute reservation with headquarters at Towoac, Colorado, and consisting mostly of the Weminuche band. Tragically, of the 810,000 acres the Southern Ute reservation originally encompassed, only 307,000 acres were left after homesteading.

Meanwhile, a small additional allotment of trust land and fee-patent land, eventually totalling close to six-thousand acres, was created at White Mesa, south of Blanding, Utah, for a group of Weminuche Utes, who were determined to remain close to their native Blue Mountains. Today these lands, with about three hundred Utes living on them, are administered as part of the Ute Mountain Ute reservation.

From Sorrow, The Sun

Very much borne of the longing and sorrow spawned from the tragedies of the nineteenth century, the Utes in the late 1890s or early 1900s adopted the Sun Dance, a curing ceremony of the Arapaho people of the Great Plains. Along with the Bear Dance, it is one of only two major dances that the Utes still routinely perform. The Sun Dance is still held in mid-summer, according to Plains tradition, when the buffalo are fat, the chokecherries are ripe, and a full moon rises as the sun sets.

The purpose of the Sun Dance has traditionally been the "Vision Quest," a state of grace during which a warrior is purified and may have encounters with the spirit world. A successful Sun Dance is also meant to help bring plentiful herds of buffalo, deer, antelope, and elk. Among some of the Plains Indians, the Sun Dance often included self-mutilation, a practice avoided by the Utes.

In preparation for current-day dances, a tree is cut and its bark and branches, except for a short branch near the top, are removed. The resulting pole is set

Chief Ignacio

Colorado Historical Society

upright into a hole, after a buffalo skull, willow branches, and other sacred items are fastened to the remaining branch. A shelter of brush is then built around the pole, with an opening left to the east as an entrance. The resulting enclosed area is then partitioned to give each dancer a place of privacy.

Only Ute men dance, believing that as they are cured, they gain the power to cure others. The dance lasts three days and nights, while the dancers take no food or drink. The Utes believe that by emptying their bodies of all food and water, they empty themselves of impurities and evil.

At the beginning of the Sun Dance, a drummer takes up a beat and singers begin the sacred songs. The dancers, wearing only breech clouts and each with his body painted with markings unique to him, move toward the sacred pole, their eyes always upon the buffalo skull and other sacred objects above. As they move toward the pole, each blows an eagle-bone whistle and shakes rawhide rattles with sacred white eagle feathers attached. After reaching the pole, the dancers move backwards to start the cycle over again. If a dancer finally collapses from exhaustion, dehydration, or heat stoke, it is considered a sacred moment by all, for it is believed that at that moment the dancer is touched by the Great Spirit.

The Present

In 1950, under the Indian Claims Act of 1946, the Utes won judgements totalling forty-three million dollars from the United States government for lands taken from them in the 1800s, monies which were invested and now represent a significant source of tribal revenue. Additional tribal income is derived from energy leases on tribal property, as well as tourism, while personal income is derived largely from farming and livestock production.

In the early 1970s, the Utes, collectively numbering roughly twenty-five thousand people as of the 1980 census, also won a court judgement that they own significant historic water rights, potentially invaluable in a dry region where water is at a premium. For the Utes in southwestern Colorado, claims to these rights may be settled in return for the construction of two massive Federal water projects. One, the Dolores project, has been built. Another, the enormous Animas-La Plata project, is currently embroiled in controversy and may be blocked because of the U.S. Endangered Species Act and the threat the project may represent to endangered fish in the San Juan and Colorado rivers.

82

THE ONLY TRUE PEOPLE

Casa Rinconada, Chaco Culture National Historic Park

Mel Burnett

Suggested Reading

Ambler, J. Richard. *The Anasazi: Prehistoric People of the Four Corners Region.* Museum of Northern Arizona, Flagstaff. 1977.

Anderson, Douglas and Barbara. *Chaco Canyon: Center of a Culture.* Southwest Parks and Monument Association, Globe. 1981.

Baars, Donald L. *The Colorado Plateau: A Geologic History.* University of New Mexico Press, Albuquerque. 1983.

Bahti, Tom. *Southwestern Indian Tribes.* K.C. Publications, Las Vegas, NV. 1968.

SUGGESTED READING

Barnes, F.A. and Pendleton, Michaelene. *Prehistoric Indians: Their Cultures, Ruins, Artifacts, and Rock Art.* Wasatch Publishers, Inc., Salt Lake City. 1979.

Carlson, John B. "America's Ancient Skywatchers." National Geographic Society. March 1990.

Chapin, Frederick. *Land of the Cliff Dwellers.* University of Arizona Press, Tucson. 1988. (Originally published Boston, 1892.)

Cordell, Linda S. *A Prehistory of the Southwest.* Academic Press, Inc., Orlando. 1984.

Cordell, Linda S. "Why Did They Leave and Where Did They Go?" *Understanding the Anasazi of Mesa Verde and Hovenweep.* School of American Research Press, Santa Fe. 1985.

Crampton, C. Gregory. *Land of Living Rock.* Alfred A. Knopf, Inc., New York. 1972.

Cushing, Frank H. *The Nation of the Willows.* Northland Press, Flagstaff. 1965. (Reprint of late-1800s account of a visit to the Havasupai.)

Delaney, Robert W. *The Ute Mountain Utes.* University of New Mexico Press, Albuquerque. 1989.

Delaney, Robert W.; Jefferson, James; and Thompson, Gregory C. *The Southern Utes: A Tribal History.* Southern Ute Tribe, Ignacio. 1972.

Diamond, Jared. "The Accidental Conqueror." Discover. Family Media Publications, December 1989.

Dobyns, Henry F. and Euler, Richard C. *Wauba Yuma's People.* Prescott College Press, Prescott. 1970.

Dutton, Bertha P. *American Indians of the Southwest.* University of New Mexico Press, Albuquerque. 1983.

Euler, Robert C. *The Paiute People.* Indian Tribal Series, Phoenix. 1972.

Gilpin, Laura. *The Enduring Navajo.* University of Texas Press, Austin. 1988.

Gunnerson, Dolores A. *The Jicarilla Apache.* Northern Illinois University Press, De Kalb. 1974.

Hughes, J. Donald. *American Indians in Colorado.* Pruett Publishing Company, Boulder. 1977.

Hughes, J. Donald. *Story of Man at Grand Canyon.* Grand Canyon Natural History Association, Grand Canyon. 1967.

Iliff, Flora G.. *People of the Blue Water.* University of Arizona Press, Tucson. 1985. (Reprint of Iliff's original late-1800s journal.)

Lavender, David. *The Southwest.* University of New Mexico Press, Albuquerque. 1980.

Marsh, Charles S. *People of the Shining Mountains.* Pruett Publishing Company, Boulder. 1982.

Martin, John. *The Havasupai.* Museum of Northern Arizona, Flagstaff. 1986.

Matlock, Gary. *Enemy Ancestors.* Northland Press, Flagstaff. 1988.

McKinney, Whitney; Hart, E. Richard; Zeidler, Thomas. *History of the Shoshone-Paiutes of the Duck Valley Indian Reservation.* Institute of the American West and Howe Brothers. 1983.

Noble, David Grant (Editor). *New Light On Chaco Canyon.* School of American Research Press, Santa Fe. 1984.

Page, Jake; Page, Susanne. *Hopi.* Harry N. Abrams, Inc., Publishers, New York. 1982.

Peterson, Kenneth Lee. "At Last!: Why the Anasazi Left the Four Corners Region." Canyon Legacy, Journal of the Dan O'Laurie Museum, Moab. 1989.

Pike, Donald G. and Muench, David. *Anasazi: Ancient People of the Rock.* Crown Publishers, Inc., New York. 1974.

Reichard, Gladys A. *Navajo Medicine Man Sandpaintings.* Dover Publications, Inc., New York. 1977.

Rock Point Community School. *Between Sacred Mountains: Navajo Stories and Lessons from the Land.* Rock Point Community School, Chinle, AZ. 1982.

Rockwell, Wilson. *The Utes: A Forgotten People.* Sage Books, Denver. 1956.

Spencer, Robert F.; Jennings, Jesse D., et al. *The Native Americans.* Harper & Row, Publishers. New York.

Terrell, John Upton. *The American Indian Almanac.* T.Y. Crowell Co., New York. 1974.

Thompson, Laura, and Joseph, Alice. *The Hopi Way.* Russell & Russell, New York. 1944.

Trimble, Stephen. *The Bright Edge: A Guide to the National Parks of the Colorado Plateau.* Museum of Northern Arizona, Flagstaff. 1979.

Underhill, Ruth. *The Navajos.* University of Oklahoma Press, Norman. 1956.

Velarde Tiller, Veronica E. *The Jicarilla Apache Tribe.* University of Nebraska Press, Lincoln. 1983.

Wenger, Gilbert R. *The Story of Mesa Verde National Park.* Mesa Verde Museum Association, Mesa Verde. 1980.

Wood, Nancy. *When Buffalo Free the Mountains: The Survival of America's Ute Indians.* Doubleday & Company, Inc., Garden City. 1980.